CRAFT
★ SPIRITS ★

CRAFT SPIRITS

Eric Grossman

DK | Penguin Random House

Project Editor Martha Burley
Project Art Editor Vicky Read
US Editor Rebecca Warren
US Consultant JT Robertson
US Senior Editor Shannon Beatty
Pre-Production Producer Rebecca Fallowfield
Producer Stephanie McConnell
Jackets Team Francesca Young, Harriet Yeomans
Creative Technical Support Sonia Charbonnier
Managing Art Editor Christine Keilty
Managing Editor Stephanie Farrow
Art Director Maxine Pedliham
Creative Director Mary-Clare Jerram
Illustrations Vicky Read
Photography William Reavell

First American Edition, 2016
Published in the United States by DK Publishing
345 Hudson Street, New York, New York 10014

Copyright © 2016 Dorling Kindersley Limited
DK, a Division of Penguin Random House LLC

16 17 18 19 20 10 9 8 7 6 5 4 3 2 1
01–280241–Apr/2016
All rights reserved.

Published in Great Britain by
Dorling Kindersley Limited.

A catalog record for this book is available
from the Library of Congress.

ISBN 978–1–4654–4384–7

DK books are available at special discounts when purchased in bulk for sales promotions, premiums, fund-raising, or educational use. For details, contact: DK Publishing Special Markets, 345 Hudson Street, New York, New York 10014 SpecialSales@dk.com

Printed and bound in China

A WORLD OF IDEAS:
SEE ALL THERE IS TO KNOW
www.dk.com

Contents

Introduction

Featuring the best craft spirits in the world, this book shows you the producers to watch, the spirits to try, and the cocktail techniques to master. Each bottle has its own unique story to tell, and is made with a passion and an attention to detail that warrants the "craft" title.

What are Craft Spirits?

It is difficult to categorize craft spirits for many reasons—mainly because there are few official authorities regulating what distilleries can produce and how spirits are marketed. Although some spirits, such as Cognac, are quality-controlled by regulatory bodies, producers often identify their spirits as "craft" without explaining what that means, or disclosing key details about their product.

This book presents more than 250 top-tier craft spirits from all over the world, helping you to choose the best from an intimidating range. Although no two are identical in style and approach, all of the producers have a similar commitment to detail and quality, and a transparent philosophy that ensures each bottle delivers an unparalleled experience.

A Matter of Size

Craft distilleries usually start small, making top-notch spirits in tiny batches, and develop a devoted audience who clamor for more. Soon, these producers need to decide whether to expand to keep up. Some believe that a producer can only create the best spirits when making them in a limited, tightly controlled fashion, and for many producers one of the greatest challenges is striking a balance between meeting demand and maintaining consistency from batch to batch. However, distilleries of all sizes can entrust Master Distillers or Blenders with making sure every batch meets the highest standards.

For these reasons, this book includes a balance of small, upstart companies who limit their production volume and make spirits in tiny batches to best

control the quality of the final product. However, a selection of medium-sized, more established craft distilleries are included too—these have expanded to meet demand, but still produce high-quality spirits featuring distinctive characteristics.

People Power

Every spirit in the book has a person, or group of people, behind it. Any producers that have anonymous ownership have been omitted from the selection. A large proportion of the distilleries in the book are fully independent so maintain complete control of their production process. However, there are also several distilleries that have been acquired by larger companies but that still adhere to their original methods and levels of quality. Although some believe that producers must stay fully independent to be truly "craft," many leading craft producers have embraced the opportunity to work with larger companies whose support—both financial and intellectual—helps them to be more experimental and innovative.

Care in the Process

All craft producers have an extreme commitment to quality, which manifests itself in different ways. Many employ painstaking techniques, some of which are rooted in time-honored traditions, and won't compromise their vision or ethos in the name of efficiency or shortcuts. Artisanal processes, such as grinding or macerating ingredients—actions automated by larger companies—are often achieved by hand. Some producers embrace a "farm-to-bottle" ethos, supporting communities and sustainability by using local ingredients.

With *Craft Spirits* as your guide, discover the world's most respected producers. Find out how to create incredible infusions and develop your very own signature cocktails. Cheers!

What is a **craft spirit**? How is it made? Starting with the origins of alcohol, these pages take you through the story of the modern craft spirits **revolution**—showing you how innovators and trailblazers all over the world have **shaken up** the spirits industry. Uncover the secrets behind the most awarded and mysterious liquors on earth and find out how producers **distill, blend, and age** spirits to get the desired results. Packed with expert advice about tasting, serving, and infusing, these pages will help you **make the most** of what you drink and get you into the spirit.

GETTING IN THE SPIRIT

Distilling: a Potted History

From the Latin word *de-stillare* for "trickle down," distillation is the process of separating liquids by evaporation and condensation. Its origins are unclear, but experts believe it dates back as far as 2,000 BCE, and evidence exists of early distillation in Egypt, China, and Mesopotamia.

Then and Now

Distillation is the simple process of separating alcoholic liquors from fermented materials, and was originally used for medicinal purposes.

Today, the process hasn't changed much—producers create spirits in a very similar way, by boiling a low-proof alcoholic ferment to distill choice vapors that can be manipulated and condensed to create liquor.

With every passing century, technological breakthroughs have enabled distillers to be more efficient and specialized, so that they can create unique spirits to meet the demands of a most thirsty public.

BCE

2100

Some scholars believe that liquor originates in China in the Xia Dynasty (2100–1600 BCE), when legend has it that Du Kang cooks sorghum seeds inside a hollow tree stump. In China, alcohol is known as the "water of history"—you can trace stories of spirits back to nearly every period in Chinese history.

800

Around 800 BCE, primitive distilled alcoholic beverages are produced throughout Asia. In the Caucasus, a spirit called Skhou is made from kefir, and in India, Arrack is made from palm sap or rice with molasses.

300

In 400–300 BCE, Aristotle suggests the existence of spirit distillation when he writes: "Seawater can be made potable by distillation as well and wine and other liquids can be submitted to the same process."

CE

200

Historians believe that the alembic still is invented in Egypt in 200–300 CE by Zósimo of Panoplies, an alchemist, and his sister Theosebeia. Allegedly, the pair go on to invent many stills and reflux condensers.

800

The first documented scientific studies on distillation date to this century. Persian alchemists and scientists, such as Jābir ibn Hayyān and Muhammad ibn Zakariya al-Razi (also known as Geber and Rhazes), make great advancements.

1100

The first certain evidence of the distillation of alcohol dates back to the world's first medical school, Schola Medica Salernitana (School of Salerno) in 1100.

The copper **pot still** dates back to **200 CE**, yet its design remains **similar** to this day

Copper
pot still

Two American gentlemen show off their highly prized illegal moonshine in New York City in the 1920s.

London's widespread **gin consumption** in **the 1700s** forces Parliament to pass five acts to **control it**

1900s

There are significant advancements in areas such as chromatography (an important measurement technique), blends, and infusions, allowing producers to refine products and create balanced spirits. Prohibition hits the USA.

1800s

Soon after achieving independence, the United States sees a widespread production of spirits thanks to a surplus of corn. Spirits become an important part of American life; in the 1820s, Americans consume 7 gallons (32 liters) of alcohol per person annually.

1600s

As production and distribution spreads, spirit consumption moves away from being purely medicinal. The British Parliament passes legislation to encourage the use of grain for distilling spirits. In 1733, over 10 million gallons (38 million liters) of gin are produced in the London area.

1500s

Although it was developed much earlier, brandy—from the Dutch *brandewijn* ("burnt wine")—becomes the first western spirit to be commercially distilled, and is widely used in trading throughout Europe.

1500

German alchemist Hieronymus Braunschweig publishes the first book solely about distillation: *Liber de arte destillandi* (The Book of the Art of Distillation). Many more alchemists and physicians are inspired to follow suit.

1250

The medieval Florentine alchemist Taddeo Alderotti develops fractional distillation in 1250. Alderotti reveals the production of Aqua Vitae: he is the first to describe the process of immersing a coil in cold water to condense vapors.

Prohibition in the United States

From 1920 to 1933, Prohibition enforced a ban on the sale, production, import, and transportation of alcoholic beverages in the United States. Most large-scale producers were shut down, and many individuals opted to produce alcohol illegally. Due to their strength, distilled spirits became more popular than wine and beer. Despite it having happened a century ago, Prohibition still affects the way US distilleries create their products, and pre-Prohibition cocktails—many of which feature in this book—are entrenched in bar lexicon all over the world.

Distillery raids were common in US cities during the Prohibition era.

Talking 'bout a Revolution

With an ever-growing commitment to quality and provenance, craft producers and small-batch distilleries have revitalized the industry. Find out how pioneers are shifting the global focus away from a handful of enormous companies.

The Movement

As with any global trend, it is difficult to pinpoint the origins of the rise of craft spirits. In America, there are at least ten times more micro-distilleries operating today than there were a decade ago, and—despite myriad barriers and regulations—other countries are following suit.

> Upstart craft distilleries are **changing** the way people **choose their spirits** at stores and bars **around the globe**

New producers come from a variety of backgrounds—from home enthusiasts with no formal training to industry veterans who broke away from established distilleries to forge their own path—and all share a desire to carve out their own corner of the booming market. Here are the international trends that are uniting the movement as it spreads across the world.

Heritage Techniques to the Fore

Some say the modern craft distilling movement began as an off-shoot of micro-brewing, begun in the 1970s in England and in the 1980s in America. As outdated government regulations and licensing restrictions relaxed, small distilleries began popping up all over the world, with a focus on heritage recipes and historically faithful methods. Global consumers have paid close attention, reigniting an interest in locally made, artisanally produced spirits.

From Farm to Bottle

The earliest examples of what we call craft spirits can be traced back to the American West Coast in the early 1980s, when distilleries like Anchor and St. George began producing whisky and vodka, respectively. Soon, micro-breweries were following suit, applying the same artisanal methods which were revolutionizing beer to the production of spirits. More recently, there is a growing trend of "farm-to-bottle" distilleries, where distilleries oversee every step of the process, from growing the grains to bottling the finished spirit.

Size Matters

From a family kitchen to a Second World War aircraft hangar, micro-distilleries are cropping up in unexpected places all over the world. Unique distillery locations have transformed how some view the spirits industry, inspiring and empowering adventurous people to try their hand at distilling. This shift is evident in South Africa—although craft spirits are relatively new there, micro-distilling has grown rapidly, especially among amateur enthusiasts who want to produce fruit brandies at home. In Japan, small teams of producers have set up tiny distilleries, aiming to replicate the success and quality of traditional Scotch whisky.

Native Ingredients

From vodka made with gourmet Swedish potatoes to mezcal made from mountain-harvested silver agave plants, native ingredients often serve as the centerpiece of award-winning products. Producers are competing with one another to see who can source the most exceptional ingredients— gathering cloudberries in the Arctic and baobab fruit from trees in Africa.

Remote Locations

Many distilleries use their remote, unique locations as a selling point. Australia is currently enjoying an explosion in the craft spirits sector, and the wonders of the modern spirit and shipping industries make it possible for a consumer in Western Canada to enjoy a gin made with water from a river in Western Australia. It certainly is exciting, by any measure, to see how these spirits allow consumers to enjoy a taste of the unknown.

The Science Behind the Craft

Every spirit starts with a raw ingredient that goes through several stages of transformation. The main stages are fermenting, in which the alcohol is created, and distilling, in which this alcohol is separated and condensed in myriad ways to create a spirit.

Preparing

Distilled spirits are produced from an array of raw materials, including grapes, potatoes, and grains (see pp18–19). Depending on the spirit and the technique, producers may grind the raw material into a coarse meal to break it down and release starch, which converts into sugars. Alternatively, non-grain materials, such as potatoes, sugar cane, and fruits, are cooked or juiced. The resultant sugars are then mixed with pure water and cooked to produce a mash, before being transferred to the mash "tun"—the fermenting container.

- -

Fermenting

Once producers have prepared the mash, it is ready for fermentation, which is a natural process of decomposition. Producers need to add yeast for fermentation to occur—yeast feeds on the sugar in the prepared mash, in the process producing alcohol and carbon dioxide (CO_2). Processes vary from producer to producer, and from spirit to spirit; some producers allow natural fermentation to occur, usually in open containers, while others use scientifically controlled methods. Fermentation can take anywhere from a few hours to several weeks, with the end product resembling a low-alcohol liquid that is similar to wine or beer—known as the "wash."

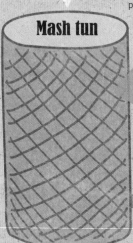

1 Producers select their base ingredients according to the spirit they are producing, and their preference

2 Producers prepare the base ingredients in different ways, including grinding and/or cooking them to form a mash

3 Producers add yeast to the mash in the tun so that it ferments to produce a low-proof wash

Mash tun

5 The wash is pumped into the still and vaporizes in the steam (see pp20–21)

Still

Distilling

In basic distillation, a liquid made of two or more parts is separated with the addition and subtraction of heat. The fermented alcoholic wash is heated to boiling point in a still. Elements of the wash vaporize and condense at various temperatures—the distiller selectively extracts these vapors to create a new mixture that can be bottled, or manipulated further with filtering, blending, aging, or flavoring. This basic procedure is the same around the world for most spirits—but different stills function in different ways (see pp20–21).

6 Vapor flows into the condenser, where it cools to become a crude spirit that is ready for repeat distillation and then filtering

Filtering

After several distillations, spirits undergo a basic filtration to eliminate large particles and sediment. Most spirits also pass through charcoal or carbon filters in order to achieve purity and flavor. Some distillers eschew this step to retain "congeners"—elements such as by-product alcohols and tannins that can lend additional character and flavor to a spirit. After filtering, the spirit may be bottled, blended, or aged.

7 The filtered spirit is ready for bottling, or blending and aging (see pp16–17)

4 A heating element floods steam into the still

Blending and Aging

Blending

Once a spirit has been distilled, producers may choose to blend it with other spirits. Whisky, brandy, Cognac, and aged rum often go through a blending process, where producers blend two or more spirits of the same variety. Many of the world's most sought-after spirits are blends, each with its own unique formula. A wave of forward-thinking producers—many of whom are featured in this book—are creating new craft spirits by experimenting with the blending process.

The Art of the Blend

If distilling is a science, then blending is an art. The process involves great skill—traditional whiskies are often produced in the same manner as vodka, but it is the blending (and aging) process that gives the spirit its unique character and multitude of expressions.

Part of a Master Blender's challenge is to select from a variety of components, choosing each at the right age to combine the various flavors and characteristics into the best expression. A symphony serves as an ideal metaphor for the blending process—the Master Blender is akin to a composer who must understand the instruments and the best way to combine them, in varying strengths, to create a pleasing piece of music. The blender must also produce a consistent finished product—the most successful blended spirits are consistent from year to year.

Blenders usually add in smaller quantities of aged, premium spirits

Young, high-proof spirits are usually the base spirit in the blend

The Master Blender chooses from a selection of base spirits

Most producers conduct the blending process on a small scale, in a lab-like environment, then apply their findings on a larger scale by marrying barrels or containers together to achieve the right blend.

When the blend is ready, it is scaled up to make larger batches

Whisky Blends Explained

Of all the spirits, whisky most frequently undergoes the blending process. Good-quality blended whiskies are perfect for mixing in cocktails. Many producers must deal with strict—sometimes complicated—regulations, and it is helpful to know what some of the industry's most common blending terms represent.

Blended Scotch Whisky
This is a blend of one single-malt Scotch whisky with one or more single-grain Scotch whiskies. All whiskies of this nature—as well as in Canadian and Irish blends—must be aged for at least three years.

Blended American Whiskey
This contains a minimum of 20 percent straight whiskey, which must be at least three years old. The aging requirement does not apply to other whiskies in the blend.

Blended American Rye Whiskey
This contains a minimum of 51 percent straight rye whiskey. Blended bourbon whiskey must contain the same proportion of corn whiskey.

Aging

The aging process is commonly associated with dark spirits. However, forward-thinking producers are departing from tradition by barrel-aging unexpected spirits, such as gin. Resembling young whisky in color and flavor, aged gin has become the darling of craft distillers.

The Whisky Barrel

The clear, harsh liquid that emerges from the still is called moonshine. Most whiskies are aged in oak barrels to mature and take on a darker hue, and historically the legal minimum for aging whisky is three years. During the aging (or "mellowing") process, whisky is said to "breathe" in the barrel, cultivating its distinct flavor, aroma, and color. Aging rounds out raw whisky's myriad abrasive notes, yielding a smoother, more desirable expression of the spirit. During this process, a portion of the alcohol evaporates, and this loss of liquid is famously known as the "angels' share."

Bourbon must be aged in new, charred American white oak barrels.

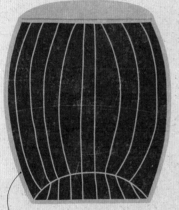

These barrels have charred interiors— bourbon gains color and flavor from the caramelized sugars in this wood

Scotch is usually aged in older bourbon barrels.

These old bourbon barrels serve as a neutral vessel for the new Scotch to age slowly, developing complex flavors ranging from fresh flowers to a smoldering campfire

Irish whiskey is usually aged in old sherry barrels.

These barrels are made from Spanish oak and impart flavors of nuts and dried fruit to whiskey— due to the influence of sherry

Agave Spirits

According to Mexican law, tequilas must be aged for a minimum of two to three weeks to produce tequila blanco, and more expensive and prized tequilas must age for longer (see right). Producers impart character to their tequilas by using a wide variety of aging vessels, from sherry barrels and Scotch barrels to French oak barrels.

Aging Tequila

Tequila blanco
at least 2 weeks

Tequila oro
at least 2 months

Tequila resposado
up to 1 year

Tequila añejo
1–3 years

Brandy and Cognac

Fine brandies are often aged in oak barrels that soften the base spirit's abrasive notes while adding flavors and aromas. Cognac might be the most strictly regulated spirit with regards to the aging process—French authorities ensure that each product is labeled according to the duration and style of aging in Limousin oak barrels (see right).

Aging Cognac

VS (very special) blend
at least 2½ years
(the youngest Cognac)

VSOP (very superior old pale) blend
at least 4 years
(the youngest Cognac)

XO (extra old) blend
at least 10 years
(the youngest Cognac)

The Base Ingredients

As with any food or drink, the quality of a spirit is dependent on the quality of its base ingredients. These ingredients often appear clearly on a bottle's label, as many craft producers are keen to emphasize their fresh, local, and sustainable choices. Here is a selection of ingredients that form the foundation of most spirits.

Corn

Many American producers have made their name by producing corn whiskey. Instead of allowing it to rot or sit in storage, farmers often sell surplus corn to distilleries, who then process it and distill it to create spirits. The corn imparts a distinctive flavor and mild sweetness that is noticeable in many whiskies and bourbons.

Used for Whisky, vodka, moonshine

Fresh corn kernels are dried and processed ahead of fermentation

Barley

Barley is a resilient grain with more protein and fiber than the likes of wheat and rye. It is also the best-suited grain for malting, and is therefore a key component in whisky, especially Scotch. While producers often use barley to give body to a clear spirit, it is not as commonly used as other grains due to its strong flavor.

Used for Whisky, vodka, gin, shochu

Barley is sometimes malted (sprouted then dried) to gain more flavor and help convert its starch to sugar

Rye

While some rye-based spirits do feature notes of rye bread, many experts feel the grain has a slight bitterness or spiciness not found in corn-based products. As a result, producers are more likely to blend rye whiskey rather than selling it straight, and most ryes are made from a mash that's at least 51 percent rye, with corn and malted barley forming the rest of the mash.

Used for Whisky, vodka

Rye is primarily grown in cold-weather areas, making it popular with distillers in North America and Eastern Europe

Wheat

Due to their strong and nutty flavor, wheat-based spirits are not always the most popular, especially as growing numbers of people suffer from gluten intolerances. However, many distillers opt to add a little wheat to their recipes in order to impart a slight sweetness and a bread-dough aroma, and are keen to distinguish the kind they use, such as spring or winter wheat.

Used for Whisky, vodka, gin

Wheat is milled to remove the outer husks (bran) before it is added to the mash tun

Potato

Notoriously difficult to use in distilling, potatoes are highly perishable and release more impurities than most ingredients. However, full-bodied potato-based vodkas are flooding the market, and are popular because of their creamy mouthfeel. More so than most components, potatoes convey a true sense of place—the different varieties producers use offer a direct reflection of varying terrain and climate.

Used for Whisky, gin

Potatoes are boiled and crushed into a purée or "soup" in order to break down their starch enough to ferment

Fruits

Although they are best known for their use in wine and cider, grapes, apples, and pears form the base of many craft spirits. Natural sugars from fruit impart a clear sweetness into spirits such as brandy, Armagnac, Calvados, and pisco. Small producers are creating spirits that evoke the remote farms, rolling hills, and bucolic countryside from where so many of these fruits are harvested.

Used for Whisky, vodka, gin, brandy, Cognac, pisco, grappa

Williams (aka Bartlett) pears are the most commonly used variety

Botanicals

Gin is essentially vodka that has been distilled with botanicals to impart flavor and aroma. Classic botanicals, such as juniper berries, wormwood (the key component of absinthe), and coriander, have stood the test of time and are found in recipes the world over. Others, such as frankincense and cassia root, are unknown to most consumers and serve as new toys for distillers to play with. In addition to gin and absinthe, a new wave of flavored craft spirits is on the rise, such as cinnamon whisky and pink-peppercorn vodka.

Used for Gin, absinthe, liqueur

Cinnamon

Fennel seeds

Wormwood

Agave

Although tequila is commonly thought to be the king of Mexican spirits, it is only one member of a family of liquors that draws flavors from the agave plant, of which there are more than 200 species. These succulent plants flower only once, and are often harvested from hard-to-reach areas for processing and distilling.

Used for Agave spirits, such as mezcal, sotol, and tequila

Traditionally, the heart of the plant—the piña—is roasted, crushed, and fermented

Sugar Cane

Sweet, tropical sugar cane forms the backbone of most rums and cachaças. Traditionally, fresh sugar cane is harvested (often from exotic rainforests and lush jungles) and then crushed to obtain juice. Producers boil the juice in order to extract crystallized sugar, and what remains is the backbone of most rums: molasses (which retains about half of the sugar from the cane juice). There are dozens of varieties, and producers disagree about the sweetest and purest option.

Used for Rum, cachaça, vodka

The stalks of this tall grass contain a sucrose-rich liquid. The fibrous parts are not used in distilling.

The Stills

The two main types of stills are pot and column varieties. Distillers choose which to use according to preference and the needs of particular spirits. There are also regulations to guide them—for instance, by law, producers are permitted to distill Cognac only in pot stills.

Spirit and Polish

Many craft producers use different techniques or equipment to enhance quality. Traditionally, producers use small-batch pot stills for flavor-rich spirits, such as brandy, mezcal, and single-malt Scotch, and column stills for neutral spirits, such as vodka and white rum.

Distilling in the Pot Still

Small in size, traditional pot stills are favored by purists looking to create quality spirits with a nod toward history and authenticity. These dynamic stills—usually made from copper—are labor-intensive, energy-consuming affairs, requiring cleaning and resetting between batches, although modern versions have made technological advancements.

Pot stills make use of simple distillation—a mixture is heated by the boiler, and vaporizes into separate parts, due to the different boiling points of water and alcohol. The vapors condense and are collected as a liquid end product. Single distillation results in a strong, crude spirit, so spirits are usually distilled more than once.

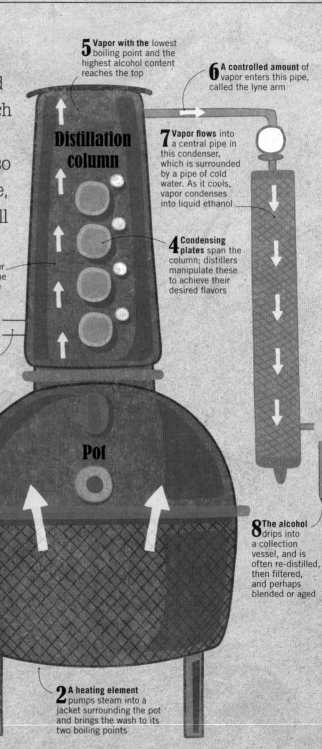

Distillation column

Pot

5 **Vapor with the** lowest boiling point and the highest alcohol content reaches the top

6 **A controlled amount** of vapor enters this pipe, called the lyne arm

7 **Vapor flows** into a central pipe in this condenser, which is surrounded by a pipe of cold water. As it cools, vapor condenses into liquid ethanol

4 **Condensing plates** span the column; distillers manipulate these to achieve their desired flavors

3 **The alcohol** and water vapors rise up into the column; most condense and fall into the pot

1 **The fermented** base (a low-proof alcohol known as the "wash") is added to the pot by a tube

8 **The alcohol** drips into a collection vessel, and is often re-distilled, then filtered, and perhaps blended or aged

2 **A heating element** pumps steam into a jacket surrounding the pot and brings the wash to its two boiling points

Distilling in the Column Still

Modern column stills are generally thought to be more efficient and economical than pot stills because they require one distillation as part of a continuous process. Multiple chambers allow for exact separations within a complex liquid, known as fractional distillation. This gives distillers great flexibility, although critics claim that the output can lack character and complexity. Column stills also produce a higher concentration of alcohol in the final distillate, compared to pot stills, which produce low-strength batches.

Some producers use steam distillation in a column still—this involves passing steam through ingredients to distill alcohol or extract essential oils from plant materials.

4 **The mixture** of alcohol vapors and steam rises to the top of the column

9 **At the required** strength, vapor condenses at the top and runs through a water-cooled condenser

1 **The wash** goes through the analyzer column into the rectifier column, where it goes through tubes and ends up inside the analyzer

3 **The wash** boils, and vapors rise through a series of plates inside the analyzer column. Depending on their temperature and density, some vapors may become trapped in the plates

10 **The liquid** is collected, and often re-distilled, then filtered, and perhaps blended or aged

2 **Steam is fed** into the base of the analyzer, and meets the wash on the column's perforated plates

7 **The wash** vaporizes, forcing the alcohol up the still, through long curved pipes

5 **The spent** wash runs down and exits from the base

Analyzer column

6 **The hot** vapors enter the rectifier at the bottom, where they meet the wash

Rectifier column

8 **Any solids** in the wash fall to the bottom and are recycled or discarded

A Taste for the Good Stuff

Once you've chosen a lovingly made craft spirit, the next step is to try it. Some craft spirits work well with mixers, but most are best on their own or with nothing more than ice or a dash of water. Most producers recommend drinking their spirits at room temperature, but if you prefer, try adding a single ice cube.

How to Appreciate

Take these steps to have the best tasting experience possible. Have some water on hand to refresh your tastebuds between sips. If you struggle to recognize the characteristics of a spirit, add an ice cube or a dash of water to open it up, but keep in mind that cooling a spirit may dull the aroma and flavor.

When tasting multiple spirits, nibble a plain cracker between tastings to reset your palate.

If you are tasting multiple expressions of the same spirit, start with the youngest and lightest, then move on to stronger, darker varieties. Leave a little in each glass so you can go back and forth to discern the differences.

1 The pour Pour a small amount into the glass of your choice (see below). Resist temptation and "drink with your eyes" first—examine the liquid, hold it up to the light, note the colors (which often correlate to flavors), and gently swirl it around the glass to release the aromas.

Most spirits don't need to breathe: a spirit that sits too long may experience evaporation and lose character.

2 The nose With your nose about 2in (5cm) above the glass, inhale slowly. Gently swirl and, as your senses adjust, inhale again closer to the liquid. Your olfactory sensors will respond to certain components and affect the way you taste the spirit.

3 The sip Start with a small sip, and let the liquid roll around your tongue. Note the feeling on your tongue and in your throat and nose. Take another sip. Savor it and reflect on whether it suits your palate. If it is abrasive, add an ice cube or a dash of water or soda.

The Right Glass

There are a few tasting vessels that can help you to get the most out of your tasting experience. Be sure to clean your glasses thoroughly, as particles or residue can affect the tasting experience. Avoid using your glasses straight from the dishwasher, as the warm surface might heat up the liquid and alter its characteristics.

Snifter

Spirit Brandy, Cognac, whisky, and aged spirits, such as rum and tequila

Why? The short stem encourages you to cradle the glass in your hand, helping to warm—and therefore open up—the drink. The large bowl allows swirling (to release aromas), and the small mouth traps aromas.

Cradle the large bowl in your hand

Old Fashioned

Spirit Whisky, vodka, gin

Why? This is the opposite of the snifter, as the thick base is designed for holding ice, though it can also be used for a neat pour. These are ideal for spirits on the rocks, or drinks that require muddling.

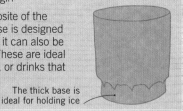

The thick base is ideal for holding ice

Flavor Wheel

There are thousands of characteristics to look for in spirits, so tasting can seem overwhelming. Use this flavor wheel to help pinpoint your observations.

Rums are made from natural sugar cane and molasses so fall squarely into the sweet section of the wheel.

Fruit-based spirits such as brandies and Cognacs are likely to fall into the fruit section of the wheel.

Gin often features botanical flavors, so if you are tasting gins, the vegetal section is a good place to start.

Whisky flavors vary from bottle to bottle—the earth section of the wheel helps to identify complex flavors.

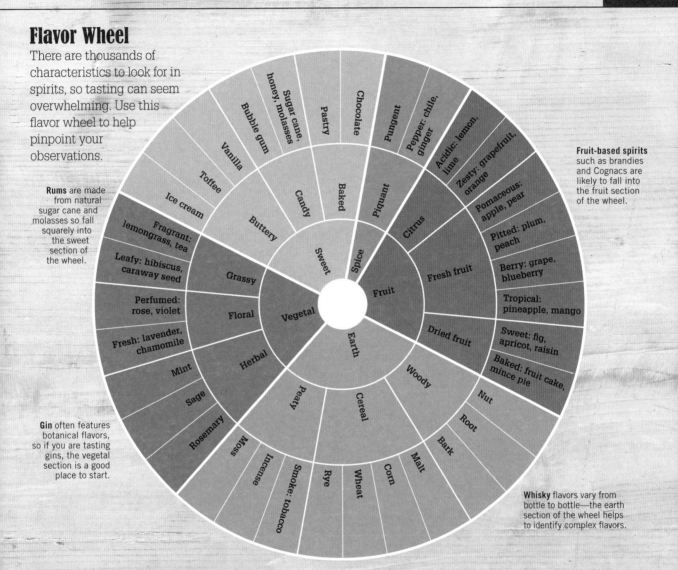

Cordial

Spirit Brandy, Cognac

Why? This classic, elegant design is ideal for after-dinner drinks. Typically thinner and more delicate than a small wine glass, the stem allows you to smell and consume the liquid without warming it up too quickly.

Hold the glass by the stem to avoid heating the liquid

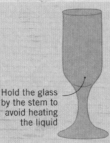

Glencairn

Spirit Whisky

Why? This glass is the most similar glass to the nosing glasses used by Master Blenders. The wide bowl shows off colors and helps expose aromas, and the tapered mouth allows for easy consumption.

The wide bowl makes it easy to discern colors

Infusing Spirits

Infusing spirits with flavor is a very simple way to craft your spirits and gets great results. Use this technique and the creative recipes in this book to enhance a bland or nondescript spirit.

What you need

- 4 cups (1-liter) airtight jar, sterilized
- fine kitchen strainer
- cheesecloth or coffee filter
- 3 cups (750ml) base spirit
- your flavoring of choice

1 Gather all your equipment. Thoroughly wash all of your flavoring ingredients. You could also use small jars, making several infusions from the same bottle.

2 Prepare your ingredients. For lemon vodka, peel five lemons, and use a knife to remove excess white pith. Place the peel in the base of your jar.

4 Shake the jar lightly a few times. Examine it to ensure no impurities, such as pips or pith, are inside. Store in a cool, dry place away from sunlight.

5 Check your infusion daily, shaking lightly to distribute the flavors. After three days, taste it every day until you achieve the desired flavor.

3 Fill the jar with the base spirit, in this case vodka. Lightly stir with a wooden spoon to distribute the infusing ingredients. Cover the jar tightly.

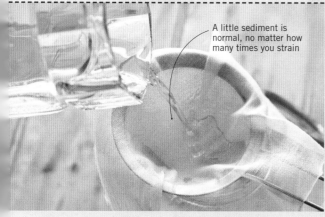

A little sediment is normal, no matter how many times you strain

6 When the infusion is ready, transfer it into a pitcher; pour into the clean jar using your strainer. Repeat, using the cheesecloth, and serve.

INGREDIENT KNOW-HOW

Follow the infusing recipes in each chapter of this book, maximizing the quality and purity of your infusion with these tips.

- **Air, heat, and large remnants** are your enemy; store your infusion in an airtight container, and strain well.
- **To maximize shelf life**, keep your homemade infusion in the fridge.
- **The base spirit sets the foundation** for your infusion. Start with a less expensive bottle—settle on a good-quality, middle-priced option. The higher the proof, the more flavor you can get from the infusion ingredients.
- **Thanks to its neutrality**, vodka is the most common base spirit. Start with a light spirit; finding the right balance with dark spirits is challenging.
- **Use the freshest ingredients**. Wash all ingredients thoroughly; chop and slice if you like, but discard any elements that you wouldn't eat, such as stems, cores, and leaves.
- **Dried fruit is a breeze**—the flavors are not as bright as fresh fruit, but the finished product's plump, boozy fruit is an additional treat.

TIME IT RIGHT

Refer to these timing guidelines, keeping in mind that the best way to judge when your infusion is ready is by trying it and checking that it suits your palate.

- **Herbs, chile peppers, vanilla pods, cinnamon sticks:** 1 to 3 days
- **Melons, berries, stone fruits, citrus:** 3 to 5 days
- **Vegetables, ginger, apples, pears:** 5 to 7 days
- **Dried spices:** 7 to 14 days

Bittersweet Symphonies

Bitters and simple syrups bring the same complexity to cocktails as salt, pepper, and spices give to food. While not core ingredients, these extras can elevate and intensify complex flavors and enhance bitter or sweet notes.

Classic Bitters

Intense and highly concentrated, bitters are extracts of ingredients such as flowers, herbs, and fruits, dissolved in alcohol or glycerin. Originally for medicinal use, these little bottles are key components of any bar. Classic bitters enhance taste through aroma, and help to counteract acidity and harsh notes in spirits.

Peychaud's

Bitters, 35% ABV

PRODUCER Sazerac Company, Louisiana, USA. Founded in 1830.

Peychaud's bitters date back to New Orleans in 1793, when they were created by Antoine Amedie Peychaud as a cure-all tonic. Peychaud began mixing it into his brandy toddy—widely considered one of the earliest known cocktails. Lighter and less bitter than most classics, Peychaud's offers hints of cherry, clove, and nutmeg. It is a vital component in Sazerac and Old Fashioned cocktails.

Angostura

Bitters, 44.7% ABV

PRODUCER House of Angostura, Trinidad. Founded in 1824.

Named after a small Venezuelan town, Angostura bitters have a secret recipe that dates back to 1824, when they were used as a medicinal tonic. In 1870, the company relocated to Trinidad, and the prestigious product is now found in bars around the globe. It has a classic, herbal flavor and bitter notes, and several classic cocktails call for it by name, including the Manhattan.

Making Simple Syrup

This clear sweetening agent is typically made with white sugar, but you can also try brown for a caramelized taste and color.

1 In a large saucepan, bring **2 cups water** to a boil over medium heat.

2 Stir in **2½ cups white sugar** until it dissolves. Remove from the heat.

3 Cool and transfer to a sterilized, airtight jar or bottle, and store in the fridge. It will keep for approximately two weeks. Add **1 tbsp vodka**, if desired, to double its shelf-life.

The next level To flavor, add approximately 2 tbsp of fruit, herb, or nut extract, such as almond, banana, mint, or cherry.

Craft Bitters

Craft producers have transformed traditional bitter or bittersweet flavors to create a kaleidoscope of tongue-tingling artisanal varieties.

Bitters and simple syrups are the **magic potions** that add complexity to cocktails

Spicy bitters feature various fiery flavors, including chile and black pepper.

Spiced chocolate bitters add depth to a White Russian

Chile bitters add a kick to any vegetal drinks, and work with tequila

Fruity bitters are the widest range—from sweet–tart rhubarb, to citrus and berry.

Tart citrus bitters work in light, fresh gin, vodka, or tequila drinks

Cherry bitters add sweetness to whisky-based cocktails

Herbal bitters encompass classic herbs and Asian-influenced galangal or makrut lime.

Mint bitters can enhance a Mojito or Rum and Ginger

Coriander bitters transform a Mai Tai or gin cocktail

Vegetal bitters, such as celery, cucumber, or bell pepper, add balance to sweet cocktails.

Improve your Bloody Mary cocktail or a gin and tonic with a couple of dashes of celery bitters

Serving With Style

Even the most exquisite drink just isn't a cocktail if you don't serve it with panache. Pay your respects to the art of the cocktail by serving your drink in the correct glass, with complementary extras that can elevate the entire experience.

All About the Glass

Glassware has evolved in order to complement every kind of cocktail. Some vessels are meant to fit certain volumes of liquid, others help to control temperature or release aromas. A speciality store can sell dozens of shapes and sizes, but for the home consumer, only a handful of styles is really necessary, and it is easy to get creative with what you already have—for example, by using a clean jam jar as a quirky collins glass replacement.

Martini (aka Cocktail)

Cocktails Martini, Manhattan, Cosmopolitan, Blood and Sand

The sloping sides display a stick of olives nicely and prevent the ingredients from separating

A long stem keeps warm hands away from the cold drink in the bowl

Perhaps the most iconic glass design, the Martini glass exudes elegance. Perfect for shaken or stirred drinks without ice (served "up"), the stem prevents your hands from warming the drink, and the conical shape opens up the liquid, thereby enhancing the drink's aromas.

Double Old Fashioned (aka Rocks)

Cocktails Negroni, Sazerac, White Russian, Old Fashioned, Mai Tai, Caipirinha

These vessels are traditionally used for cocktails that are mixed in the glass, rather than a shaker. A traditional old-fashioned glass should be 6–8fl oz (175–240ml) in volume, and a double old-fashioned glass holds twice the volume.

The wide mouth is perfect for grated garnishes

A sturdy, flat bottom makes it easier to muddle ingredients

The Crafty Garnish

Bartenders often let their creative juices flow by garnishing with the likes of pickled, crystallized, and dehydrated fruits and vegetables. The best garnishes take the experience up a notch by adding an extra dimension to the cocktail.

Flamed Citrus Peel

Impart a smoky citrus aroma garnishing with a flamed peel. Prepare a 1–2in (2.5–5cm) round of peel. With care, hold a lit match 3in (7.5cm) above the cocktail. Hold the peel colored-side down, another 3in (7.5cm) above the lit match. Twist and squeeze the peel over the lit match, then rub the peel around the rim of the glass.

Smoky Ice Cubes

Liquid smoke is an inexpensive, easy-to-use product with a smoky flavor. When making ice cubes, add a few drops to each cube; as the cubes melt into your drink, they impart a smoky flavor that complements strong, bold cocktails, such as a Manhattan or an Old Fashioned.

How to Rim Your Glass

Adding a sweet, salty, or spicy coating to the rim of a glass transforms a cocktail's appearance, mouthfeel, and flavor profile.

1 Rub the rim of a glass with a citrus wedge, or dip the vessel in simple syrup, agave syrup, or the main spirit from your cocktail.

2 Place the glass face-down on a plate covered in your desired coating.

The next level Start with coarse salt or crystallized sugar. You could play around with chili powder, sweet- or savory-smoked salt, and ground cinnamon.

Coupe
Cocktails Daiquiri, Sidecar, Gimlet, Corpse Reviver No. 1

Collins (aka Highball)
Cocktails Bloody Mary, Mojito, Gin Fizz, Gin Sling, Paloma, Absinthe Frappé

Historically used for sipping Champagne, this wide brim is best suited to fragrant cold cocktails

Less top-heavy, and therefore less prone to spilling than the similar Martini glass, the coupe evokes a bygone era when formality reigned in the world of cocktails. The liquid should reach to the top of the glass, ensuring that the drinker's nose stays in close proximity to the aromas.

The elegant stem makes this glass easier to hold than the Martini

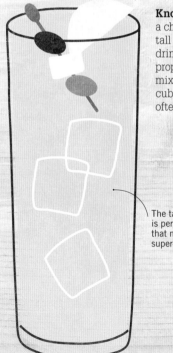

Known in some circles as a chimney-style glass, this tall vessel is used for cold drinks containing a large proportion of non-alcoholic mixers served over lots of ice cubes. Modern bartenders often favor a large jar.

The tall collins glass is perfect for drinks that need to be served super-cold with ice

Vodka is a **clean spirit** that boasts subtle characteristics ranging from grassy and herbal to **sweet and spicy**. First made in Poland and Russia more than a thousand years ago, the spirit is now **popular all over the world**. Traditionally, vodka is made by the distillation of fermented cereal **grains** or potatoes, although—as shown on these pages—modern producers are turning **convention on its head** by distilling grapes, whey, honey, and more. The most versatile of all spirits, vodka can provide a **blank canvas** for experimentation, making it easy for you to play with full-flavored infusions or to **create your own** versions of classic vodka cocktails.

VODKA

Arbikie

Vodka, 43% ABV

DISTILLERY Arbikie Distillery, Angus, Scotland. Founded in 2014.
PHILOSOPHY A single-site operation, this distillery focuses on traditional farm-to-bottle techniques.

The spirit The team farms the potatoes on site and picks and ferments them at the peak of creaminess. The resulting "wash" is distilled in a copper still with water that has filtered through the local Angus Hills.

The taste Black pepper is present from the nose to the finish, with hints of white chocolate and pear. The mouthfeel is smooth and creamy.

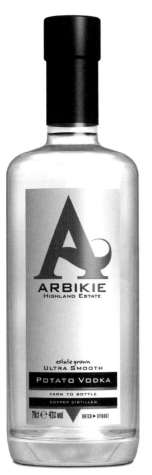

Babička

Vodka, 40% ABV

DISTILLERY Starorežná Distillery, Prostejov, Czech Republic. Spirit launched in 2007.
PHILOSOPHY Reviving the magic and mystery of a 500-year-old Czech "witches' brew."

The spirit The distillery applies a six-step process to natural ingredients such as hand-picked wormwood, young Moravian corn, and water from 10,000-year-old springs. Filtering through coal ensures smoothness.

The taste This vodka features a soft and clean texture and a subtle sweetness that is offset by the light notes of fennel and anise.

Bainbridge Organic

Vodka, 40% ABV

DISTILLERY Bainbridge Organic Distillers, Washington, USA. Founded in 2009.
PHILOSOPHY Proud to be organic and sustainable, this distillery uses ingredients from fully traceable sources.

The spirit This complex vodka is made from soft white wheat, which is finely ground in batches on a daily basis. The ferment is distilled four times, and the producer takes care to ensure the spirit's signature viscosity.

The taste The vodka's aroma (citrus peels, vanilla, and fresh young herbs) yields to a smooth and lightly sweet taste, followed by a mineral-driven finish with a note of spice.

Barr Hill

Vodka, 40% ABV

DISTILLERY Caledonia Spirits, Vermont, USA. Founded in 2011.
PHILOSOPHY This distillery was founded by Todd Hardie—a beekeeper, naturalist, and farmer—so it has a deep connection to its agricultural roots.

The spirit Around 2,000lb (900kg) of raw honey makes up each batch of vodka. After fermenting for about three weeks, the resulting mead is distilled twice in custom-made stills. Each bottle is sealed by hand using beeswax.

The taste The use of raw honey imparts a distinctive, pure, and soft botanical essence to every sip.

Black Cow

Vodka, 40% ABV

DISTILLERY Black Cow, West Dorset, England. Founded in 2012.
PHILOSOPHY To diversify the output of his dairy herd, an award-winning cheesemaker uses his own unique process to make vodka.

The spirit Fresh milk is separated into curds, for cheese, and whey, for vodka. The whey is fermented into a "milk beer" that is then distilled, blended, triple-filtered, and bottled by hand.

The taste Smooth and rounded, the vodka features sweet vanilla and cinnamon notes with a warming and slightly creamy finish.

Blue Duck

Vodka, 43% ABV

DISTILLERY Deinlein Distillery, Bay of Plenty, New Zealand. Spirit launched in 2013.
PHILOSOPHY A German Master Distiller skillfully handcrafts vodka in New Zealand; a portion of proceeds goes to conservation efforts to save the namesake bird.

The spirit Without the need for additives, sugars, preservatives, or softeners, this award-winning vodka is made from 100 percent pure whey distillate. Filtered five times in local spring water, it undergoes seven distillations in a reflux copper pot.

The taste With an aroma featuring gentle notes of lemon, wheat, and straw, this vodka features hints of peppery spice and lemon, with a warm, velvety, and tingly mouthfeel.

Bootlegger 21 NY

Vodka, 40% ABV

DISTILLERY Prohibition Distillery, New York, USA. Founded in 2010.

PHILOSOPHY From his base in the scenic Catskill Mountains, an award-winning distiller creates pure-tasting spirits.

The spirit The team distills and then slowly filters 100 percent New York State corn for more than 24 hours through 800lb (360kg) of oak charcoal. The unique process, attention to detail, and lack of additives yield exceptional smoothness.

The taste Almost odorless, this gentle vodka is soft on the palate with a silky mouthfeel. The smooth and clean flavor lacks any burn or aftertaste.

The poppy is a symbol of remembrance for the soldiers who have died during wartime

The attractive and ornate decorations on the bottle honor the Art Nouveau style that was popular in the US during Prohibition

CapRock

Vodka, 40% ABV

DISTILLERY Peak Spirits Farm Distillery, Colorado, USA. Founded in 2005.

PHILOSOPHY The producers at this farm-to-bottle distillery use "clean-growing" practices to ensure the best ingredients.

The spirit The farm biodynamically grows Chambourcin grapes that are then fermented whole spontaneously (without commercial yeast). The makers then distill the ferment twice and re-distill with organic Romanian winter wheat distillate.

The taste Whole grapes contribute soft fruit tannins to a rich and oily mouthfeel. The neutral flavor is followed by a pleasingly dry and clean finish.

Cathead

Vodka, 40% ABV

DISTILLERY Cathead Distillery, Mississippi, USA. Founded in 2010.
PHILOSOPHY Reflecting the South's rich musical history, Cathead has a philanthropic approach and supports local live music.

The spirit A corn mash is distilled six times, matured in stainless steel, and run through a series of filtering processes, including through charcoal.

The taste This vodka has a clean and rich flavor profile and a smooth and sweet finish.

Charbay

Vodka, 40% ABV

DISTILLERY Charbay Distillers, California, USA. Founded in 1983.
PHILOSOPHY This family-owned distillery and winery was an early pioneer of the modern craft spirits' movement.

The spirit Charbay's thirteenth-generation Master Distiller uses 100 percent non-GMO corn. For purity, he distills the spirit to 192 proof, then gently filters it and uses a unique water process to reach 80 proof.

The taste A touch of sweetness from the corn tempers this vodka's silky mouthfeel, thick body, and warm finish.

Chase

Vodka, 40% ABV

DISTILLERY Chase Distillery, Herefordshire, England. Founded in 2008.
PHILOSOPHY This family-owned, single-estate distillery pays close attention to the entire production process—every bottle is filled and sealed by hand.

The spirit Chase grows King Edward and Lady Claire potatoes, processes them, and distills them four times in a custom-made copper batch pot. Roughly 300 potatoes go into every bottle.

The taste With a highly prized full-bodied and creamy texture, this vodka has complex flavor notes of buttery mashed potato, cinnamon, nutmeg, and ginger.

Cold River

Vodka, 40% ABV

DISTILLERY Maine Distilleries, Maine, USA. Founded in 2004.
PHILOSOPHY This "ground-to-glass" distillery performs every aspect of production, including growing the base potatoes.

The spirit The distillery mashes whole potatoes and creates a potato "soup" that is fermented into a wine. This wine is distilled and then blended with water from the nearby Cold River.

The taste Smooth and full bodied, the vodka's distinctive, complex flavor boasts creamy and starchy potato notes with hints of black pepper.

Corbin Sweet Potato

Vodka, 40% ABV

DISTILLERY Sweet Potato Spirits, California, USA. Founded in 2009.
PHILOSOPHY Widely considered one of the world's first farm-to-bottle distillery, these pioneers make a range of sweet potato spirits.

The spirit About 50 people contribute to producing each bottle—grinding, cooking, fermenting, and distilling locally grown sweet potatoes. The process is exceptionally labor-intensive.

The taste You can trace this silky spirit's primary flavors—slightly nutty with caramel undertones—directly back to the sweet potato.

Death's Door

Vodka, 40% ABV

DISTILLERY Death's Door Distillery, Wisconsin, USA. Founded in 2005.
PHILOSOPHY This is a community-minded producer that supports the local economy by sourcing sustainable grains and local ingredients.

The spirit Wheat, barley, and corn are distilled "grain-in" (without any additives). The grains pass through an intricate filtering process that produces an exceptionally smooth and rounded spirit.

The taste A rich and buttery mouthfeel gives way to a slight sweetness with subtle notes of vanilla and hints of pepper spice.

HOW TO ENJOY The taste and mouthfeel suits straight sipping.

English Spirit

Vodka, 54% ABV

DISTILLERY English Spirit Distillery, Cambridgeshire, England. Founded in 2009.
PHILOSOPHY Proud to be an independent distillery producing a diverse range of artisan spirits in very small batches.

The spirit Comprised of only three ingredients—East Anglian sugar beet, yeast, and water—this remarkable vodka is single-distilled in exceptionally small batches using a copper pot still.

The taste English Spirit has a clean and slightly oily mouthfeel with complex flavor notes—ranging from vanilla and caramel to fennel.

Fair

Vodka, 40% ABV

PRODUCER Fair Vodka, Cognac, France. Spirit launched in 2009.
PHILOSOPHY Embracing a one-of-a-kind collaboration between French distillers and Andean farmers, combined with a unique production process.

The spirit Organic, gluten-free quinoa—sourced in a Fairtrade manner from the fertile volcanic soil of the Andes Mountains—is shipped to Cognac, where it is distilled five times.

The taste This vodka offers a delicate, fruity aroma, light peppery flavor notes, and a slightly oily, medium-body finish.

Fire Drum

Vodka, 40% ABV

DISTILLERY Tasmania Distillery, Hobart, Australia. Spirit launched in 2013.
PHILOSOPHY Showcasing the natural elements of one of the world's most pristine environments.

The spirit This small-batch vodka is made from two of Tasmania's finest ingredients, malted barley and pure mountain water. It is distilled twice in a traditional copper pot and then filtered through charcoal.

The taste A unique expression of the spirit, this vodka features the smooth and sweet notes of malted barley and vanilla.

Florida Cane (St. Augustine)

Vodka, 40% ABV

DISTILLERY St. Augustine Distillery, Florida, USA. Founded in 2014.
PHILOSOPHY Utilizing the best of Florida's agriculture, the team makes everything by hand to ensure the flavors of each ingredient can shine.

The spirit The labor-intensive, handcrafted process requires almost no filtering after pot distillation, allowing the unique character of local sugar cane to stay at the forefront of the flavor.

The taste Soft with a pleasant natural sweetness, the vodka has a long finish with notes of white pepper, anise, and green apple.

Freimut

Vodka, 40% ABV

DISTILLERY Freimut Spirituosen GmbH, Wiesbaden, Germany. Founded in 2013.
PHILOSOPHY Using only natural raw materials, Freimut produces a vodka with character that enriches the taste of serious cocktails.

The spirit This additive-free "mono-grain" vodka is handmade using only spring water and North German "Champagne" rye malt from a family-owned organic malthouse.

The taste An aromatic spirit with rye-bread and roasted-hazelnut flavors.

HOW TO ENJOY
This is a perfect choice for an extra-dry Martini.

Hangar 1

Vodka, 40% ABV

DISTILLERY Hangar 1 Vodka, California, USA. Founded in 2001.
PHILOSOPHY Engaging in every aspect of the production process, from sourcing fine wine grapes and grains to distilling and bottling.

The spirit This is one of America's most popular vodkas, made from a blend of pot-distilled wine grapes and column-distilled American grain. The vodka began production in an old Second World War aircraft hangar, hence its name.

The taste Perfectly balanced, this vodka is floral on the nose, with hints of Asian pear and honeysuckle. The mellow taste quickly transitions to a dry and lightly perfumed finish.

Hanson of Sonoma Organic

Vodka, 40% ABV

DISTILLERY Hanson Distillery, California, USA. Founded in 2013.
PHILOSOPHY This family-owned and -run distillery makes 100 percent grape-based organic vodka in small batches.

The spirit The distillery harvests organic grapes, then crushes and ferments them into a wine, which it then distills in both a pot and a 50-plate column still.

The taste Nicely balanced on the nose and palate, this silky vodka rewards you with an enjoyably lengthy finish.

Hophead

Vodka, 45% ABV

DISTILLERY Anchor Brewing & Distilling Company, California, USA. Founded in 1993.
PHILOSOPHY These innovators helped to spark the modern craft spirits' movement in San Francisco and beyond.

The spirit This is one of America's most decorated breweries, now experimenting with many hop-based spirits. Two types of aromatic dried hops go into the distillery's small copper-pot stills to create its vodka.

The taste This vodka captures the fresh and aromatic character of hops without any bitterness. With similar notes to beer and gin, it contains grapefruit, grassy, and floral flavors.

Ironworks

Vodka, 40% ABV

DISTILLERY Ironworks Distillery, Nova Scotia, Canada. Founded in 2008.
PHILOSOPHY Distilling by hand in small batches, Ironworks uses natural ingredients that are as fresh and local as possible.

The spirit The production team grinds Annapolis Valley apples, mixes them with German white wine yeast, and ferments them for six to eight weeks. After 17 hours of double distillation, the spirit is then filtered and blended with purified water.

The taste This vodka has a smooth texture and gentle flavor with hints of sweet apple and butterscotch.

Hangar 1 Vodka was founded in California, USA, in 2001. Its first distillery was housed in a Second World War aircraft hangar—the inspiration behind the company's name. Using a rare method for producing vodka, Hangar 1 distills fresh wine grapes in a pot still and American wheat in a column still, then blends them together.

What's the story?

Hangar 1 is inspired by Old World distilling and uses fresh local ingredients. Going by the strapline "Fresh Picked California Vodka," the distillery applies traditional European eau de vie techniques with Midwestern wheat and ripe California wine grapes. The result is a smooth vodka with a softening hint of fruit essence.

Head distiller Caley Shoemaker and the team also create flavored varieties by infusing the vodka base with fresh fruit, and then distilling the vodka in a pot still. They use seasonal fresh fruit and spices grown in the US—including makrut lime and buddha's hand citron.

What's next?

In 2016, Hangar 1 opened a new visitor center to celebrate the history of the surrounding community of Alameda and its Naval Air Station. The center includes an outdoor grove, botanical garden, and store overlooking the San Francisco Bay. Visitors can listen to Shoemaker amongst others discussing the vodka process and sample various products—both from the core everyday line-up as well as new small-batch flavored spirits.

Right Hangar 1 Vodka's flagship products are made with this custom-made copper pot still with two columns.

Hangar 1 VODKA

Left Hangar 1 complements this vintage logo with a modern Apothecary-style bottle design. Both are inspired by Hangar 1's workshop—a hub for experimentation.

Above The labeling line of bottles of Hangar 1 Straight Vodka, which is the primary product of the brand's core line.

Who is behind it?

A self-proclaimed "spirits nerd" and one of the few female distillers in the vodka industry, **Caley Shoemaker** is fascinated by how the chemistry of distilling affects the quality, texture, and flavor of the final product. An innovative Head Distiller, she draws on inspiration from the Bay Area's abundant seasonal ingredients to create her products.

Shoemaker is **inspired** by the Bay Area's abundant **seasonal** ingredients

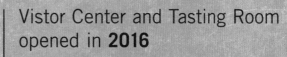

FOUNDED IN
2001

Vistor Center and Tasting Room opened in **2016**

CRAFTED
1 batch at a time

4 vodkas
in the **core range**—Straight, Mandarin Blossom, Makrut Lime, and Buddha's Hand Citron

Jewel of Russia

Vodka, 40% ABV

PRODUCER Jewel of Russia, Moscow, Russia. Spirit launched in 1999.

PHILOSOPHY Using traditional methods to preserve the authentic character of classic Russian vodka.

The spirit The producer distills hard-winter wheat, rye, and water from deep wells five times. The spirit is filtered five times through paper, sand, and charcoal made from peach and apricot pits.

The taste This full-bodied yet smooth vodka features an understated sweetness with a touch of minerality and mildly spicy rye notes.

Kalevala

Vodka, 40% ABV

DISTILLERY Northern Lights Spirits, North Karelia, Finland. Founded in 2012.

PHILOSOPHY This organically certified micro-distillery uses the highest-quality ingredients.

The spirit The production team distills organically grown wheat five times and mixes it with water that comes fresh from the distillery's own well.

The taste With a nose that's dominated by citrus, this silky vodka features a crisp, full flavor with a warm and spicy finish.

Karlsson's Gold

Vodka, 40% ABV

DISTILLERY Spirits of Gold, Gripsholm, Sweden. Founded in 2007.

PHILOSOPHY Honoring vodka's heritage, the distillery uses a traditional method that retains the ingredients' rich natural flavors.

The spirit The use of highly prized Virgin New potatoes—roughly 15lb (8kg) go into each bottle—creates a flavorsome, handcrafted, single-distilled, and unfiltered vodka.

The taste Rich and full-bodied, this vodka has a distinctive flavor and vibrant character.

Konik's Tail

Vodka, 40% ABV

DISTILLERY Polmos Białystok, Białystok, Poland. Spirit launched in 2010.

PHILOSOPHY Named after the wild ponies of Poland's primeval forest, Konik's Tail is crafted in limited quantities from three distinct grains.

The spirit Carefully sourced spelt, golden rye, and early-winter wheat ensure the integrity of this vodka. It is produced following Polish traditions that date back more than 600 years.

The taste With ripe graininess and a rich full-bodied mouthfeel, this is a distinctive vodka. It has spicy and nutty flavors, with a gentle citrus finish.

King Charles

Vodka, 40% ABV

DISTILLERY Charleston Distilling Co., South Carolina, USA. Founded in 2009.

PHILOSOPHY Using hand-selected grains from a local farm, this distillery mills, mashes, ferments, distills, ages, blends, and bottles on site.

The spirit The Master Distiller uses a corn–rye mix for the mash bill and leaves the grain in through several stages of the distillation process to ensure maximum flavor.

The taste The primary ingredients— smooth corn and peppery rye—provide a balance of sweet and spice.

The Lakes

Vodka, 40% ABV

DISTILLERY The Lakes Distillery, Cumbria, England. Founded in 2014.

PHILOSOPHY In a remote corner of England, traditional production methods produce clean-tasting spirits that exude a sense of place.

The spirit Made with fresh water from the River Derwent (made famous by the poet William Wordsworth), this triple-distilled, wheat-based vodka is distilled in a small, handmade copper pot still.

The taste With a smooth and silky mouthfeel, the spirit yields a rich aroma that features a hint of wheat.

Napa Valley

Vodka, 40% ABV

DISTILLERY Napa Valley Distillery, California, USA. Founded in 2009.

PHILOSOPHY In the heart of America's Wine Country, this innovative distillery makes vodka in a brandy still using Sauvignon Blanc wine.

The spirit The production team distills Napa Valley Sauvignon Blanc wine in a copper pot that was designed for premium brandy-making. The spirit is distilled until it reaches the high proof necessary for vodka.

The taste Full of flavor and character with a large aroma, this smooth vodka features notes of green apple and vanilla.

New Deal

Vodka, 40% ABV

DISTILLERY New Deal Distillery, Oregon, USA. Founded in 2004.

PHILOSOPHY Making a variety of quality spirits —both traditional and offbeat—in small batches.

The spirit Local, coarse-milled wheat ferments for five days, then undergoes a rough distillation, followed by a still run in a 22-plate copper still. The hands-on, in-house process allows the distillery to control the results.

The taste This clean, easy-drinking vodka has hints of wheat, with a floral nose and a pleasingly round mouthfeel.

North Shore

Vodka, 40% ABV

DISTILLERY North Shore Distillery, Illinois, USA. Founded in 2004.

PHILOSOPHY Chicago's first post-prohibition distillery is making flavorsome spirits in small batches using the best raw materials available.

The spirit The staff uses Midwestern wheat and corn, the interplay of which yields a unique flavor. The use of filtered water from Lake Michigan gives the spirit a distinguished texture.

The taste Clean, crisp, and smooth, this versatile and award-winning vodka has a round texture with a slightly sweet finish.

Prince Edward

Vodka, 40% ABV

DISTILLERY Prince Edward Distillery, Prince Edward Island, Canada. Founded in 2007.
PHILOSOPHY In a self-sustaining and eco-friendly way, two female distillers utilize the rich harvest of the island in partnership with local farmers.

The spirit Roughly 15lb (8kg) potatoes go into one bottle of Canada's first potato vodka. The team distills the spirit three times before bottling.

The taste The starchy potatoes impart a creamy, smooth texture and sophisticated taste.

A fruity vodka, this suits straight sipping.

okanagan spirits

VODKA

Craft Distilled In B.C.

750 ml.   40% alc./vol.

The lighthouse is a symbol of Prince Edward Island—lighthouses of many shapes and sizes dot the coastline

The Canadian flag has pride of place on the bottle—all ingredients in the vodka are grown and produced in the country

Okanagan Spirits

Vodka, 40% ABV

DISTILLERY Okanagan Spirits, British Columbia, Canada. Founded in 2004.
PHILOSOPHY To produce a selection of speciality spirits, made from 100 percent local fruit, without additives, chemicals, or artificial flavors.

The spirit The staff distills a mixture of world-class fruit from British Columbia in a European-made copper pot still, then blends it with pure spring water. It is made without artificial flavoring, coloring, or extracts.

The taste This elegant vodka features lightly fruity notes and a smooth finish.

Silver Tree (Leopold Bros.)

Vodka, 40% ABV

DISTILLERY Leopold Bros., Colorado, USA. Founded in 1999.
PHILOSOPHY This family-owned and -operated distillery employs traditional pre-Prohibition era methods and natural ingredients.

The spirit Colorado barley passes through the distillery's traditional malting room and kiln. Along with potato and wheat, the malted barley goes into open-air wooden fermentation tanks and a 30ft (9m) column still for the final distillation.

The taste Soft and gentle due to a long, cool fermentation, this vodka has some creaminess from the potato.

Snow Leopard

Vodka, 40% ABV

DISTILLERY Polmos Lublin, Lublin, Poland. Spirit launched in 2010.
PHILOSOPHY This is the world's first spelt vodka; a portion of proceeds goes toward snow leopard conservation efforts.

The spirit Made with small batches of the nutty spelt grain and water drawn from the distillery's artesian well, this vodka is distilled six times, passing through a state-of-the-art, continuous column still.

The taste This vodka's lightly floral aroma nicely complements its rich nut and spice flavors, with a touch of creamy vanilla and honey.

Purity

Vodka, 40% ABV

DISTILLERY Purity Vodka Distillery, Scania, Sweden. Founded in 2002.
PHILOSOPHY Using natural ingredients, old-school Swedish traditions, and an intricate process to produce a smooth organic spirit.

The spirit Organic winter wheat and malted barley are placed in a unique copper-gold still. The product is then distilled an incredible 34 times, during which 90 percent of the liquid is lost—as a result, no filtration is necessary.

The taste Notes of white chocolate, rosebuds, and lime complement this vodka's rich and malty elements. It has a gentle and pleasing mouthfeel.

Spring44

Vodka, 40% ABV

DISTILLERY Spring44 Distilling, Colorado, USA. Founded in 2010.
PHILOSOPHY This distillery's core values—quality, sustainability, authenticity, and transparency—are exemplified by a commitment to using water from just one spring.

The spirit The vodka is comprised of 60 percent Rocky Mountain artesian mineral spring water (sourced at an elevation of 9,000ft/2,700m), and 40 percent distilled grain-neutral ethanol made from American-grown corn.

The taste After a lightly sweet and dry start, with hints of slate and rainwater, the vodka provides a creamy and velvety texture, with a long and spicy finish.

Square One Organic

Vodka, 40% ABV

DISTILLERY Distilled Resources, Inc., Idaho, USA. Spirit launched in 2006.
PHILOSOPHY This family-owned spirits company creates innovative and organic products, produced with an eco-conscious mindset.

The spirit This vodka—made from organic American rye and pristine water originating in the Teton Mountains—achieves sparkling clarity with just one distillation in a four-column continuous still and one filter through micron paper.

The taste Full of flavor and character, this crystal-clear vodka offers a rich, nutty taste, with the texture of American rye.

True North

Vodka, 40% ABV

DISTILLERY Grand Traverse Distillery, Michigan, USA. Founded in 2007.
PHILOSOPHY The Master Distiller behind this 100 percent "grain-to-bottle" distillery strives for the highest-quality spirits, one small batch at a time.

The spirit Made with filtered fresh water from the Great Lakes, the vodka undergoes three runs in the still, passing through 36 plates for a total of 39 distillations.

The taste Locally grown rye lends a gentle sweetness—think fudge, egg cream, and toasted rye bread—that rolls across the palate with an exceptionally smooth finish.

Vestal

Vodka, 40% ABV

DISTILLERY Gorzelnia Rolicz, Główczyce, Poland. Spirit launched in 2008.
PHILOSOPHY Small-scale production and a connection to local terroir ensures a good-quality spirit with varying characteristics.

The spirit Using a blend of young native potatoes and quality water, Vestal distills this vodka only once, to capture exotic aromas and flavors that vary across each small batch.

The taste Depending on the vintage, sensitive palates will discern flavor notes ranging from apple, kiwi, and mint to bell pepper, tangerine, and tobacco.

HOW TO ENJOY
Vestal is the ideal base for fruity cocktails.

Unruly

Vodka, 40% ABV

DISTILLERY Wayward Distillation House, British Columbia, Canada. Founded in 2014.
PHILOSOPHY Balancing tradition with creativity, this artisan craft distillery is the first in Canada to use honey as the base for all of its spirits.

The spirit Unpasteurized and all-natural, this unique vodka is made from fresh glacier water, specialized yeast, and honey from the wild clover fields of Northern British Columbia.

The taste Full-bodied and smooth, the vodka's honey flavor is complemented by a hint of vanilla on the palate.

Watershed

Vodka, 40% ABV

DISTILLERY Watershed Distillery, Ohio, USA. Founded in 2010.
PHILOSOPHY This distillery is passionate in its support of local agriculture and industry. With a dogged commitment to perfection, it produces a range of quality spirits.

The spirit Wastershed makes a mash from local corn and cooks, cools, and ferments it. The mash is pumped into a 660-gallon (3,000-liter) still, and distilled four times. Each bottle is labeled by hand with a batch number.

The taste The faintly floral aroma gives way to a lightly sweet taste, with citrus notes and a dry, clean finish.

Whitewater (Smooth Ambler)

Vodka, 40% ABV

DISTILLERY Smooth Ambler Spirits, West Virginia, USA. Founded in 2009.
PHILOSOPHY Keen family values of quality and hard work enrich the range of spirits produced at this Appalachian distillery.

The spirit Made from local corn and wheat mixed with barley, this vodka is distilled using a pot-and-column still.

The taste This has a creamy mouthfeel, with fruit essences and a little sweetness.

Woody Creek

Vodka, 40% ABV

DISTILLERY Woody Creek Distillers, Colorado, USA. Founded in 2012.
PHILOSOPHY From farm to bottle, Woody Creek has total control over every element of its production process: everything is picked, crafted, and bottled by hand.

The spirit The team at Woody Creek strip and mash locally grown potatoes and combine them with mountain spring water. The vodka is distilled just once in custom-made artisan copper pot stills.

The taste With a fresh and inviting nose, this vodka is smooth yet robust. The silky mouthfeel yields to hints of vanilla and sweet cream.

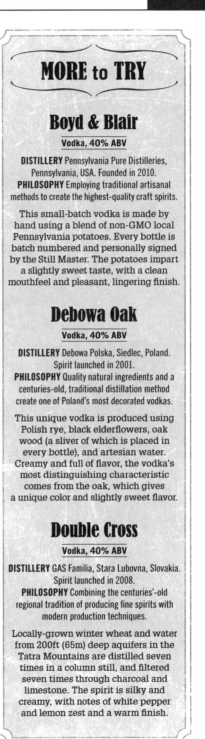

MORE to TRY

Boyd & Blair

Vodka, 40% ABV

DISTILLERY Pennsylvania Pure Distilleries, Pennsylvania, USA. Founded in 2010.
PHILOSOPHY Employing traditional artisanal methods to create the highest-quality craft spirits.

This small-batch vodka is made by hand using a blend of non-GMO local Pennsylvania potatoes. Every bottle is batch numbered and personally signed by the Still Master. The potatoes impart a slightly sweet taste, with a clean mouthfeel and pleasant, lingering finish.

Debowa Oak

Vodka, 40% ABV

DISTILLERY Debowa Polska, Siedlec, Poland. Spirit launched in 2001.
PHILOSOPHY Quality natural ingredients and a centuries-old, traditional distillation method create one of Poland's most decorated vodkas.

This unique vodka is produced using Polish rye, black elderflowers, oak wood (a sliver of which is placed in every bottle), and artesian water. Creamy and full of flavor, the vodka's most distinguishing characteristic comes from the oak, which gives a unique color and slightly sweet flavor.

Double Cross

Vodka, 40% ABV

DISTILLERY GAS Familia, Stara Lubovna, Slovakia. Spirit launched in 2008.
PHILOSOPHY Combining the centuries'-old regional tradition of producing fine spirits with modern production techniques.

Locally-grown winter wheat and water from 200ft (65m) deep aquifers in the Tatra Mountains are distilled seven times in a column still, and filtered seven times through charcoal and limestone. The spirit is silky and creamy, with notes of white pepper and lemon zest and a warm finish.

Infusing Vodka

The most neutral spirit, vodka is the easiest option for an at-home infusion. Opt for a clean, basic-flavored variety, and play around with your favorite flavors and ingredients. Follow the best method for infusing on pages 24–25.

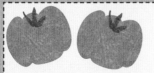

Heirloom Tomato

Pair a grassy-flavored vodka with juicy, fresh-flavored heirloom tomatoes.

What you need 1lb (450g) heirloom tomatoes, quartered; 3 cups vodka.

Infusing time 5–7 days.

The next level Throw in a handful of your fresh herb of choice—tarragon and thyme both work well.

Bubblegum

If you're a fan of bubblegum flavor, avoid the fake-tasting, processed versions on the market and make your own.

What you need 1–2 packets of any soft bubblegum; 3 cups vodka.

Infusing time 3–5 days.

The next level Use classic pink bubble-gum and add even more flavor with a handful of fresh cherries or blueberries.

Beet

Colorful beet offers a sweet yet vegetal option.

What you need 2–3 medium beets, peeled and cut into chunks; 3 cups vodka.

Infusing time 5–7 days.

The next level Experiment by adding a handful of fresh basil or the peel of one lemon (pith removed).

Tea

Tea-infused vodka adds character to many cocktails.

What you need 2–3 good-quality tea bags; 3 cups vodka.

Infusing time 1–2 days.

The next level This recipe works with most varieties of tea—black, green, jasmine, Earl Grey, and chai are all popular options. Consider adding the peel of one lime or orange for a refreshing boost of citrus, but avoid including any bitter pith.

Horseradish

For a spicy kick, use fresh horseradish; this improves a standard Bloody Mary.

What you need 2oz (60g) fresh horseradish, peeled and grated; 3 cups vodka.

Infusing time 1 day.

The next level Add ½ teaspoon whole black peppercorns to enhance the savory and spicy notes in your vodka.

Chocolate

Infuse vodka with chocolate—it works well in dessert-style cocktails.

What you need 2–3oz (60g–85g) dark chocolate, broken into pieces or 3½oz (100g) cocoa powder; 3 cups vodka.

Infusing time 2–3 days.

The next level Just as you would pair flavors with chocolate, try adding complementary ingredients into the infusion, such as the peel of one orange, pith removed; grated ginger; a vanilla pod; or a cinnamon stick.

Bloody Mary

The Bloody Mary is the world's most popular savory cocktail. According to legend, it was first shaken to life in 1921 at the New York Bar in Paris. Once considered a complex concoction, the Bloody Mary is now known as a quick and easy brunch-time favorite. Enjoy it in its classic form, or give the cocktail your own playful and creative spin.

The Classic Recipe

Savor the simple, spicy, and fresh flavors of the classic.

1 Fill a chilled collins glass with ice cubes.
2 Pour 4fl oz (120ml) tomato juice into the glass.
3 Add 2fl oz (60ml) vodka.
4 Add 1½ teaspoons fresh lemon juice.
5 Add a dash each Tabasco and Worcestershire sauce. Stir for 10 seconds.

Serve it up Season to taste, and garnish with a celery stalk, olive, and lemon wedge.

Create Your Own Signature Mix

Key Components

1 Fill your glass with **ice cubes**.
Boost the flavor by using frozen tomato juice or beef stock instead.

2 Add **4fl oz (120ml) tomato juice**.
Choose a good-quality bottled mix with concentrated flavor. For intensity, purée and strain two to three fresh tomatoes.

3 Add **2fl oz (60ml) vodka**.
Enhance the vodka's character by infusing it with chile pepper, tomato, or citrus.

4 Add **1½ teaspoons fresh lemon juice**.
Intensify the flavor—muddle two quarters of fresh lime and add a dash of citrus bitters.

5 Add a **dash each Tabasco and Worcestershire sauce**, and stir.
For an umami flavor, replace the sauces with freshly grated or pickled veggies, or even cooked shrimp.

Ice cubes

Sauces

Fresh lemon juice

Vodka

Tomato juice

Additional Flourishes

Garnish Choose a show-stopping garnish, such as a large shrimp or a lobster tail.

Seasoning Add color and flavor—try smoked salt or coarse sea salt, and paprika or ground pink peppercorns.

Bitters Add a dash or two of punchy bitters—from smoky and spicy to citrus—to create offbeat flavors.

Skewers Thread skewers or vegetable spears with fresh, pickled, or dehydrated vegetables; cubes of cheese; hard-boiled quail eggs; or candied bacon.

Craft Reinventions

Bartenders love to customize the Bloody Mary with spices, such as harissa or aleppo pepper, or heirloom vegetables, such as purple carrots or yellow wax beans. On the right are three fresh and modern takes on this savory favorite.

Beefy Bloody Bull

Shake the liquid ingredients in a shaker for 10 seconds, then pour the mixture into an ice-filled collins glass. Season with celery salt and black pepper, top with a lemon wedge, and serve.

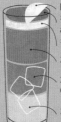

- lemon wedge
- ¾ tsp each Worcestershire and hot chili sauce
- ¾ tsp fresh lemon juice
- 2fl oz (60ml) fresh tomato juice
- 2fl oz (60ml) cold beef stock, or Bouillon
- 2fl oz (60ml) vodka

Spicy Bloody Maria

Shake the tequila, juices, and one dash of bitters and sauce in a shaker for 10 seconds. Pour into an ice-filled collins glass. Add salt, cayenne pepper, and a dash each of bitters and sauce. Serve.

- 2 dashes each of spicy bitters and hot chili sauce
- 3½fl oz (100ml) fresh tomato juice
- 1½ tsp lemon juice
- 1½fl oz (45ml) blanco tequila

◀ Blonde Mary

Shake the vodka, vinegar, a dash of bitters, tomato purée, and juices in a shaker for 10 seconds. Pour into an ice-filled collins glass. Season. Add a dash of bitters, lemon, and the skewer. Serve.

- slice of lemon with a feta and olive skewer
- 1½ tsp each pickle juice and fresh lemon juice
- 4fl oz (120ml) yellow tomatoes, puréed and strained
- 2 dashes of citrus bitters
- 1½ tsp Champagne vinegar
- 2fl oz (60ml) pepper-infused vodka

Cosmopolitan

The Cosmopolitan, or "Cosmo," was first served in the 1970s. However, it wasn't until the TV show *Sex and the City* featured the cocktail in the 1990s that the Cosmo entered the global lexicon. Love it or loathe it, this easy-to-drink and vibrant mixture appeals to fans of smooth and sweet cocktails. The classic is the perfect choice for craft reinvention.

The Classic Recipe

Fruity and sweet, the classic Cosmo is easy to make and even easier to drink.

1 Pour 3fl oz (90ml) vodka into a shaker.
2 Add 1fl oz (30ml) triple sec.
3 Pour in 1fl oz (30ml) cranberry juice.
4 Add 1 tablespoon fresh lime juice.
5 Fill the shaker with ice cubes and shake for 10 seconds. Strain into a chilled Martini glass.
Serve it up Garnish with a lemon twist.

Create Your Own Signature Mix

Key Components

1 Pour **3fl oz (90ml) vodka** into a shaker.

Opt for a flavored craft vodka, such as lemon, cranberry, orange, or pineapple.

2 Add **1fl oz (30ml) triple sec**.

Triple sec adds a fruity-yet-boozy element, but other fruit-forward liqueurs, such as craft brandy or schnapps, enhance the flavor profile.

3 Pour in **1fl oz (30ml) cranberry juice**.

Use fresh juice instead of concentrated. If it is unavailable, try other flavor-rich choices, such as grape or cherry.

4 Add **1 tablespoon fresh lime juice**.

Up the quantity to 2 tablespoons for a sharp hit that tempers the sweetness.

5 Fill the shaker with **ice cubes** and shake for 10 seconds. Strain into your glass.

For an extra-smooth texture, use chipped or crushed ice in your shaker—this allows a little ice to make it through the strainer into your glass.

Fresh lime juice
Cranberry juice
Triple sec
Vodka

Additional Flourishes

Bitters You may wish to add a few dashes of bitters. These range in flavor from lightly botanical to strong and bold.

Garnish The traditional Cosmo often features artificial colors and flavorings. Go the craft route by choosing new garnishes, such as dehydrated lime powder or frozen cranberries.

Craft Reinventions

A true Cosmo must feature sweet notes, but mixologists often introduce a spicy or sour component or natural fruit flavoring to the mix. On the right are three innovative variations that elevate the Cosmopolitan to new heights.

Sour Apple Cosmo

Mix the vodka, schnapps, fruit juices, and bitters in a shaker. Fill with ice cubes and shake for 10 seconds. Strain into a chilled Martini glass, garnish with slices of apple, and serve.

- slices of apple
- dash of sour or citrus bitters
- 1fl oz (30ml) cranberry juice
- 1 tbsp fresh lime juice
- 1 tbsp sour apple schnapps
- 1½fl oz (45ml) apple or lemon vodka

Creamy Peach Cosmo

Mix the vodka, schnapps, lemon juice, and peach juice or nectar in a shaker. Fill with ice cubes and shake for 10 seconds. Strain into a chilled Martini glass, garnish with peach, and serve.

- slice of peach
- 1fl oz (30ml) fresh peach juice or nectar
- 1 tbsp fresh lemon juice
- 1 tbsp peach schnapps
- 1½fl oz (45ml) peach vodka

◂ Spicy Pineapple Cosmo

Mix the vodka, fruit juices, and bitters in a shaker. Fill with ice cubes and shake for 10 seconds. Strain into a chilled Martini glass, garnish with pineapple and jalapeño, and serve.

- pineapple chunk and slice of jalapeño
- dash of spicy bitters
- 1fl oz (30ml) fresh pineapple juice
- 1 tbsp cranberry juice
- 1 tbsp lime juice
- 1½fl oz (45ml) jalapeño-infused or lemon vodka

The Moscow Mule was invented in 1941 at a bar in Hollywood that, legend has it, once faced a surplus of vodka and home-made ginger beer. When a Russian woman came to the bar selling 2,000 copper mugs from her father's shop, the iconic cocktail was born. Find out how to make the classic, then create your own version or try modern variations.

The Classic Recipe

One of the easiest cocktails there is, the Moscow Mule gets its "kick" from the ginger beer.

1 Pour 2fl oz (60ml) vodka into a chilled copper mug.

2 Add 1 tablespoon fresh lime juice.

3 Pour over 5fl oz (150ml) ginger beer.

4 Stir thoroughly, and pack the mug with crushed ice.

Serve it up Garnish with a lime wheel.

Create Your Own Signature Mix

Key Components

1 Pour **2fl oz (60ml) vodka** into your copper mug or glass.

Choose a craft vodka that features complementary grassy or herbal notes.

2 Add **1 tablespoon fresh lime juice**.

Pair the ginger with other full-flavored fruits, such as Meyer lemon or yuzu.

3 Add **5fl oz (150ml) ginger beer**.

For a fresh take on the spicy notes, infuse soda water with fresh ginger or tamarind pulp. Avoid sweet ginger ale.

4 Stir, and pack the mug with **crushed ice**.

You can also use pebbled ice, or make ginger-infused ice cubes, then crush them.

Crushed ice

Ginger beer

Fresh lime juice

Vodka

Additional Flourishes

Garnish Replace the lime garnish with another citrus fruit, or try a herb garnish, such as basil or thyme.

Bitters Choose spicy bitters to complement the sour citrus, or add a dash of a vinegar shrub.

Decorate Try edible seasonal flowers, such as calendula, or dehydrate banana or lemon slices for accents of flavor.

Craft Reinventions

In the new world of Moscow Mules, only one constant remains: the copper mug. Some mixologists add sweetness with fruit purées or liqueurs, and others incorporate spices for a fiery kick. Here are three recipes to transform your Mule.

Fig Mule

Stir the vodka, lime juice, agave syrup, sage leaves, and purée in a shaker for 10 seconds. Strain into a copper mug filled with crushed ice. Top up with ginger beer and garnish with fig. Serve.

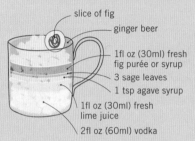

- slice of fig
- ginger beer
- 1fl oz (30ml) fresh fig purée or syrup
- 3 sage leaves
- 1 tsp agave syrup
- 1fl oz (30ml) fresh lime juice
- 2fl oz (60ml) vodka

Apple Cider Mule

Mix the vodka, cider, and juice with ¼ tsp ground cinnamon in a copper mug. Stir and fill with crushed ice. Top up with ginger beer, and garnish with the cinnamon and apple slice. Serve.

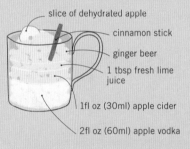

- slice of dehydrated apple
- cinnamon stick
- ginger beer
- 1 tbsp fresh lime juice
- 1fl oz (30ml) apple cider
- 2fl oz (60ml) apple vodka

◀ Blueberry Mint Mule

Muddle the mint, blueberries, and juice in a shaker. Add the vodka and shake for 10 seconds. Strain into an ice-filled copper mug and pour over ginger beer. Top with the mint and skewer. Serve.

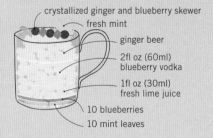

- crystallized ginger and blueberry skewer
- fresh mint
- ginger beer
- 2fl oz (60ml) blueberry vodka
- 1fl oz (30ml) fresh lime juice
- 10 blueberries
- 10 mint leaves

White Russian

The White Russian is the mother of all sweet and creamy cocktails. Thought to be an American original from the mid-twentieth century, it is very popular with those who like to drink their desserts. Vodka and coffee liqueur play starring roles in the classic, but it is fun and easy to turn the recipe completely on its head.

The Classic Recipe

Few ingredients are required for a classic White Russian, making it a great party choice.

1 Fill a chilled double old-fashioned glass with ice cubes.

2 Pour 2fl oz (60ml) chilled vodka into the glass.

3 Add 1fl oz (30ml) coffee liqueur.

4 Top up with 1fl oz (30ml) heavy cream and slowly stir. Serve.

Create Your Own Signature Mix

Key Components

1 Fill your chilled glass with **ice cubes**.

This cocktail may separate. To avoid this, use good-quality large ice cubes that melt slowly. For extra flavor, make them with milk or cold-brewed coffee.

2 Pour **2fl oz (60ml) chilled vodka** into the glass.

Neutral, clean vodkas work best, but you can liven things up with a chocolate- or cherry-flavored vodka, or infuse neutral vodka with coffee beans or cinnamon.

3 Add **1fl oz (30ml) coffee liqueur**.

Some coffee liqueurs are too sweet. Control this by making your own to taste: mix four parts each cold-brewed coffee and rum with two parts brown sugar simple syrup, and a dash of vanilla extract.

4 Top up with **1fl oz (30ml) heavy cream** and slowly stir.

Fresh, good-quality full-fat cream or milk gives the drink its velvet-like texture. You could try dairy alternatives, such as coconut milk, that can give the drink a different flavor profile.

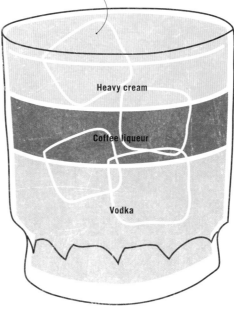

Ice cubes

Heavy cream

Coffee liqueur

Vodka

Additional Flourishes

Swirl Instead of stirring, pour the cream gently into the drink. Serve it as it swirls in the glass.

Coffee Add a dash of filter coffee or a single espresso to the drink for a caffeinated kick.

Garnish Try decorating with ground nuts, such as almonds, or grated cinnamon, nutmeg, or mace.

Craft Reinventions

Mixologists love to play with the creaminess of a White Russian by experimenting with dairy alternatives, or incorporating different flavors. Fall in love with the cocktail once more with these three modern variations.

Toasted Almond

Pour the liquid ingredients into an ice-filled shaker. Lightly stir, then strain into an ice-filled double old-fashioned glass. Gently stir, top with grated almonds, and serve.

- grated almonds
- 1 tbsp heavy cream
- 1 tbsp coconut milk
- 1fl oz (30ml) almond liqueur
- 1fl oz (30ml) coffee liqueur
- 1fl oz (30ml) vodka

Skinny Russian

Pour the vodka, coffee, agave syrup (if using), and milks into an ice-filled shaker. Lightly stir, then strain into an ice-filled double old-fashioned glass. Stir, top with nutmeg, and serve.

- grated nutmeg
- 1 tbsp skim milk
- 1 tbsp vanilla almond milk
- 1½ tsp agave syrup (optional)
- 1fl oz (30ml) cold-brewed coffee
- 1½fl oz (45ml) vodka

◀ Colorado Bulldog

Mix the vodka, coffee liqueur, and cream in an ice-filled shaker. Strain into an ice-filled double old-fashioned glass. Top up with cola, stir, and garnish with grated nutmeg. Serve.

- grated nutmeg
- 2fl oz (60ml) cola
- 1fl oz (30ml) heavy cream
- 1fl oz (30ml) coffee liqueur
- 1½fl oz (45ml) vodka

Gin is the most **full-flavored** of all clear spirits. Basically a neutral vodka that is distilled with flavors, it has a **distinctive** taste that comes predominantly from traditional botanicals, such as juniper berries, citrus peel, and coriander. The first form of gin was called **jenever**, which can be traced back to sixteenth- or seventeenth-century Holland. Perfect with tonic water, the world's favorite type of gin is **London dry**—this **juniper-heavy** variety lacks sugar and is usually higher in alcohol than other gins. Innovative craft producers use **new distilling** techniques and go to great lengths to source the most complex **botanicals** available. Explore the diversity of gin, then let your **creative juices** flow.

GIN

Adnams Copper House

Gin, 40% ABV

DISTILLERY Copper House Distillery, Suffolk, England. Founded in 2010.
PHILOSOPHY An innovative English producer that brews and distills on the same site.

The spirit To create a London Dry gin, Adnams adds six botanicals directly to the base spirit (Adnams barley vodka, made from locally grown East Anglian malted cereals) in a copper pot still.

The taste Elegant and approachable, Adnams' warming flagship gin features a classic juniper punch, followed by floral and citrus notes.

Amato

Gin, 43.7% ABV

DISTILLERY Amato Gin Distillery, Wiesbaden, Germany. Founded in 2014.
PHILOSOPHY Creating a handcrafted, small-batch, regional gin inspired by Italian flavors.

The spirit Tomatoes and a mix of hand-selected botanicals macerate for roughly 24 hours and then undergo a double distillation.

The taste Fresh scents of citrus, coriander, and peach give way to intriguing flavor notes of thyme, tomato, and cucumber.

Aviation

Gin, 42% ABV

DISTILLERY House Spirits Distillery, Oregon, USA. Founded in 2004.
PHILOSOPHY One of the Pacific Northwest's most lauded distilleries produces an award-winning spirit inspired by the great American cocktail gins of the pre-Prohibition era.

The spirit Fresh botanicals steep in high-quality American neutral grain spirit for nearly 24 hours to extract flavors. The liquid is then distilled in a custom pot still, and is blended with purified water to reach the desired proof.

The taste This complex gin gets its prized flavor from a balance of traditional and contemporary ingredients, such as cardamom, coriander, aniseed, dried sweet orange peel, lavender, Indian sarsaparilla, and juniper.

The Botanist

Gin, 46% ABV

DISTILLERY Bruichladdich Distillery, Isle of Islay, Scotland. Spirit launched in 2010.
PHILOSOPHY Self-described "progressive Hebridean distillers" use hand-foraged local island botanicals to create an innovative dry gin.

The spirit More than 30 ingredients undergo a slow distillation (to maximize flavor) in an elderly and unique Lomond still that is affectionately known as "Ugly Betty."

The taste With aromas that range from menthol to coriander, this smooth spirit delivers complex and spicy flavors.

Buss No. 509 Raspberry

Gin, 37.5% ABV

DISTILLERY Zuidam Distillers BV, Baarle-Nassau, The Netherlands. Spirit launched in 2014.
PHILOSOPHY With a somewhat unconventional approach, Buss Spirits creates artisanal flavored gins of fantastic quality.

The spirit The first product from Buss Spirits, this raspberry gin gets its distinctive flavor and color from fresh raspberries, which are macerated for up to three weeks.

The taste This soft, gentle gin offers a naturally sweet raspberry flavor. It is the perfect "gateway" gin for those who aren't usually fans of the spirit.

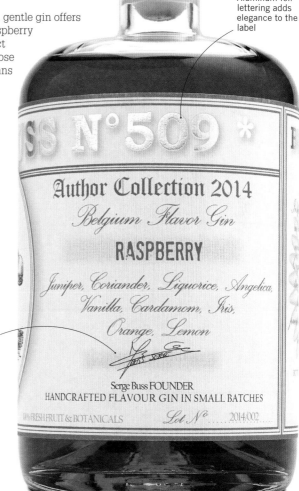

The "natural-closing" cap design is minimalistic and modern

Aluminum foil lettering adds elegance to the label

Every bottle features the signature of the founder and flavor specialist, Serge Buss

Caorunn

Gin, 41.8% ABV

DISTILLERY Balmenach Distillery, Cromdale, Scotland. Spirit launched in 2009.
PHILOSOPHY Artisanal and small batch, this gin is named after the Gaelic word for "rowan berry," a Celtic botanical that forms the backbone of the spirit.

The spirit Master Distiller Simon Buley quadruple-distills this gin in the world's only Copper Berry Chamber. Inside this copper vessel, vapor passes through four trays that are carefully packed with 11 botanicals.

The taste This gin offers a clean and crisp flavor with a long and dry finish.

Citadelle

Gin, 44% ABV

DISTILLERY Logis d'Angeac, Ars, France. Spirit launched in 1997.
PHILOSOPHY The president of Maison Ferrand, Alexandre Gabriel, creates fine gin using an eighteenth-century recipe.

The spirit This recipe calls for a complex medley of spices and a pot still. The staff triple-distills French whole-grain wheat, natural spring water, and a blend of distinct botanicals in copper pot stills. For six months of the year, the same stills are used to distill Pierre Ferrand Cognac.

The taste Soft and smooth on the palate, this subtle gin sports a long aftertaste that fully expresses the spirit's aromatic complexities.

The Cutlass (West Winds)

Gin, 50% ABV

DISTILLERY Tailor Made Spirits Company, Margaret River, Australia. Founded in 2011.
PHILOSOPHY This small distillery benefits from the abundance of rainwater in the local area and top-quality natural resources.

The spirit The base spirit for this gin is an Australian wheat grain variety, which undergoes a one-shot distillation in a copper pot still. The team adds a mix of 12 botanicals to each batch to ensure maximum flavor.

The taste This gin has a creamy white-pepper mouthfeel, accompanied by a cornucopia of unusual flavors, such as cinnamon myrtle, lemon myrtle, and Australian bush tomato.

Dorothy Parker

Gin, 44% ABV

DISTILLERY New York Distilling Company, New York, USA. Founded in 2009.
PHILOSOPHY This lauded New York City distillery creates high-quality and original spirits, celebrating the pre-Prohibition American cocktail heritage of the region.

The spirit Making this gin is a time-consuming and labor-intensive process. In a 220-gallon (1,000-liter) pot still, the producer distills a neutral-grain spirit, filtered water, and eight ingredients known as the "botanical build."

The taste This light and balanced gin features hints of juniper and citrus with deep floral notes and subtle fruit.

HOW TO ENJOY This is the perfect choice for a Martini.

Death's Door

Gin, 47% ABV

DISTILLERY Death's Door Distillery, Wisconsin, USA. Founded in 2007.
PHILOSOPHY This is a community-minded producer that supports the local economy by sourcing sustainable grains and local ingredients.

The spirit The gin's base spirit is a unique mix of three grains—wheat, barley, and corn. This distillate meshes with a simple botanical mix of juniper berries, coriander seed, and fennel through a vapor-extraction process.

The taste Fronted by a bright nose of fresh juniper, the liquid enters the palate with a creamy mouthfeel, then finishes with a cooling anise note that leaves the mouth fresh and clean.

Dutch Courage

Gin, 44.5% ABV

DISTILLERY Zuidam Distillers BV, Baarle-Nassau, The Netherlands. Spirit launched in 2004.
PHILOSOPHY This family-owned and -operated craft distillery makes use of the best ingredients from all over the world.

The spirit A unique method with separate distillations of nine botanicals in copper pot stills—from Italian iris root and Moroccan coriander to Indian licorice root—produces a fresh, dry, complex, and layered flavor.

The taste The nose is clean with fresh citrus and earthy juniper notes and a beguiling hint of spice and vanilla.

Ferdinand's Saar

Gin, 44% ABV

DISTILLERY AV Distillery, Wincheringen, Germany. Spirit launched in 2013.

PHILOSOPHY This small distillery, nestled near the vineyards that border Germany, Luxembourg, and France, makes an inviting spirit that reflects the flavors of the region.

The spirit Carefully hand-picked Riesling grapes and more than 30 botanicals contribute to this gin's complex flavor.

The taste Locally harvested ingredients, such as quince, lavender, rosehip, angelica, hop blossom, and lemon-scented thyme, complement the acidity from the grapes.

The natural cork is sealed in local beeswax

In a nod to the nearby wine-growing Saar region, traditional wine bottles are used

The product is named after the royal Prussian District Forester Ferdinand Geltz, a historical figure who also co-founded one of Germany's finest vineyards

The vintage-style label design is evocative of intricate Riesling grape vines

Elephant

Gin, 45% ABV

DISTILLERY Elephant Gin Distillery, Mecklenburg-Vorpommern, Germany. Founded in 2013.

PHILOSOPHY Inspired by the botanical discoveries of nineteenth-century African explorers, these gin pioneers donate a portion of their proceeds to African elephant conservation efforts.

The spirit A mix of 14 hand-selected botanicals—including fresh apples from the surrounding orchard and rare African ingredients such as buchu, African wormwood, and baobab—are left to macerate in a copper pot still. The staff dilutes the results with local spring water, and distills with neutral spirit.

The taste This smooth spirit stimulates the palate with a mixture of herbaceous, fruity, and spicy notes—unusual to many palates, due to the use of rare African ingredients.

Few Barrel

Gin, 46.5% ABV

DISTILLERY Few Spirits, Illinois, USA. Founded in 2011.
PHILOSOPHY This is a true "grain-to-glass" distillery—the producer ferments local grain, then distills, ages, and bottles everything in-house.

The spirit This gin starts with a high-proof neutral-flavored alcohol base, distilled from grain. The team infuses this with botanicals and then re-distills it in a dedicated gin still. For six to nine months, it ages in new American oak barrels and used bourbon and rye whiskey barrels.

The taste The mix of oak-like vanilla sweetness and spicy botanical flavor balances the spirit somewhere between a whisky and gin. Notes of cinnamon, grapefruit, vanilla, and black pepper shine through.

Filliers 28°

Jenever, 43.7% ABV

DISTILLERY Filliers Distillery, Bachte-Maria-Leerne, Belgium. Spirit launched in 1928.
PHILOSOPHY This producer distills its own malt wine in traditional copper stills—a carefully guarded family secret recipe, passed down through four generations.

The spirit Distilling jenever is a very delicate balancing act. An experienced Master Distiller observes everything from the grinding of raw materials in the milling unit to the aging of the juniper distillates in oak barrels.

The taste The pale yellow liquid carries a mild and soft flavor of grains with notes of wood, vanilla, and malt wine.

Fords

Gin, 45% ABV

DISTILLERY Thames Distillers, London, England. Spirit launched in 2012.
PHILOSOPHY Celebrating the great gin heritage of the Master Distiller, Charles Maxwell—an eighth-generation distiller.

The spirit The producer steeps nine botanicals—ranging from Chinese jasmine and Turkish grapefruit peel to Polish angelica—in neutral grain alcohol made from English wheat. Distillation takes place in a duo of unique steel pot stills made by the legendary still-maker, John Dory.

The taste Aromatic, fresh, and floral, this gin yields elegant notes of orange blossom, citrus, and juniper, with a long and smooth finish.

Geranium

Gin, 40% ABV

DISTILLERY Langley Distillery, West Midlands, England. Spirit launched in 2009.
PHILOSOPHY Celebrating decades of experience at one of Great Britain's oldest and finest gin distilleries.

The spirit This classic London Dry gin is made from ten fresh and dry botanicals, which are infused for 48 hours in 100 percent pure grain spirit made from the finest English wheat.

The taste This gin starts with a crisp and floral aroma, followed by a light flavor of juniper with sweet notes from cassia, orange, and licorice.

Gin 27

Gin, 43% ABV

DISTILLERY Appenzeller Distillery, Appenzell, Switzerland. Spirit launched in 2013.
PHILOSOPHY Distillers have collaborated with the experts behind a Swiss bar and restaurant to develop a top-quality gin at one of Switzerland's most iconic distilleries.

The spirit These are the producers behind one of Switzerland's most famous herb liqueurs, Appenzeller Alpenbitter. To make their dry gin, the team applies a mix of botanicals to a state-of-the-art distillation system.

The taste Fresh and well-composed flavor notes run the gamut from coriander and citrus zest to cinnamon, nutmeg, and cardamom.

Gin Mare

Gin, 42.7% ABV

DISTILLERY MG Distillery, Barcelona, Spain. Spirit launched in 2010.
PHILOSOPHY Using the best Mediterranean ingredients—all with completely traceable origins—in a tiny 55-gallon (250-liter) craft still.

The spirit The production team distills the ingredients individually for at least 24 hours. They peel the citrus fruits by hand and macerate them for over a year in special jars. Every batch needs 33lb (15kg) of Arbequina olives—these are blended by hand.

The taste This spirit gives off a spicy nose with herbaceous notes of pine, rosemary, tomato, and black olive. The slightly bitter finish contains traces of thyme, rosemary, and basil.

Greenhook Ginsmiths

Gin, 47% ABV

DISTILLERY Greenhook Ginsmiths Distillery, New York, USA. Founded in 2012.
PHILOSOPHY This is an award-winning, small-batch New York City distillery run by the gin-loving DeAngelo brothers.

The spirit The gin is vacuum-distilled, bringing temperatures right down. This protects delicate botanical aromas from being muted by high temperatures usually associated with the distillation process.

The taste The clean juniper and citrus nose gives way to an elegant, silky texture that lingers on the tongue and a complex and vivid finish.

G'Vine Floraison

Gin, 40% ABV

PRODUCER EuroWineGate Spirits & Wine, Cognac, France. Founded in 2001.
PHILOSOPHY Creating unique grape-based gins, this company takes a unique approach to gin.

The spirit Unlike many gins, this variety is crafted from grapes. The team enhances the base spirit with ten botanicals, including the rare vine flower from the company's legendary vineyards.

The taste This is a light, vibrantly floral gin that captures the exhilarating essence of the vineyard and the warmth of summer.

Helsinki

Gin, 47% ABV

DISTILLERY The Helsinki Distilling Company, Helsinki, Finland. Founded in 2013.
PHILOSOPHY The first independent distillery in Helsinki produces an artisanal premium gin.

The spirit The team macerates nine hand-picked botanicals (including Artic lingonberry) in Finnish neutral grain spirit for 24 hours, and then re-distills the spirit. Some of the most delicate botanicals are added to the vapor-infusion tank for extra aroma.

The taste The smooth, pleasant mouthfeel gives way to distinct bursts of fennel, coriander, orris root, and angelica, with a pinch of rose petals.

Sacred Gin

Sacred Gin is a beautifully balanced spirit. It is the triumph of distiller Ian Hart and the Sacred Microdistillery, located in his north London home. The smallest commercial distillery of its kind, Sacred has turned gin on its head by favoring vacuum distillation instead of traditional pot distillation.

What's the story?

Sacred creates a truly unique gin. To retain the individual character of each organically sourced botanical, Hart macerates each one separately in English wheat spirit. The ingredients, including whole citrus fruits, macerate for a very long time: at least four to six weeks with no air contact.

Next, Hart distills the botanicals separately in glassware vacuum stills. The air is sucked out of the stills with a vacuum pump to reduce the pressure, achieving a far lower temperature than pot distillation can. As a result, each distillate remains lush and fresh when it is blended to make the gin—think of freshly cut oranges compared to high-temperature cooked marmalade.

What's next?

In addition to Sacred's classic gin, there are also two flavored gins (Pink Grapefruit and Cardamom), vodkas and vermouths, and Rosehip Cup—an English alternative to Campari. Also in the works are sloe gin, whiskies, and new products born from trials with distilling, cask aging, and finishing.

Awarded a **Double Gold Medal** at the San Francisco World Spirits Competition, **2013**

MAY 22, 2009
First production run of Sacred Gin

2 DAYS: The time it takes **2 PEOPLE** to prepare **175lb (80kg)** grapefruit for maceration

Above The robin and the nightingale in the logo represent Sacred's location in leafy Highgate, London. The poet Keats (who wrote "Ode to a Nightingale") once lived in the area.

Left There are five custom-made stills at Sacred Microdistillery. They were all designed by Hart and made especially for Sacred by a glassware manufacturer.

Above To retain all the flavor and aroma, vapors must pass through a final liquid nitrogen-cooled condenser.

Who is behind it?

Ian Hart (far right) has always had an interest in science and was distilling from the age of 11, when he experimented with the likes of nitrogen oxide and chlorine oxide. He studied Natural Sciences at Cambridge University and worked in various fields, from cellular telephones to banking on Wall Street. Once he found himself out of a job in 2008, he set about experimenting with gin: a mere 23 experiments later, Sacred Gin was born.

Hart runs the company alongside his wife, **Hilary Whitney** (right) who was new to the drinks industry before co-founding the company.

Hernö

Gin, 40.5% ABV

DISTILLERY Hernö Gin Distillery, Ångermanland, Sweden. Founded in 2011.
PHILOSOPHY Sweden's first dedicated gin distillery is, for now, the world's northernmost. Two hand-hammered copper stills, known as Kerstin and Marit, are the soul of the distillery.

The spirit The producer distills an organic wheat spirit base twice in the copper stills. They use eight botanicals: juniper, cassia, lemon peel, vanilla, coriander, lingonberries, black pepper, and meadowsweet. The spirit matures for a month in a juniper-wood cask.

The taste Fresh juniper and woody notes shine through this round and smooth gin, with hints of honey and citrus on the finish.

Junipero

Gin, 49.3% ABV

DISTILLERY Anchor Brewing & Distilling Company, California, USA. Founded in 1993.
PHILOSOPHY These innovators helped to spark the modern craft spirits movement in San Francisco and beyond.

The spirit Made by hand in the classic London Dry gin tradition, this spirit was the first post-Prohibition craft gin to be distilled in the United States. The staff distills more than a dozen botanicals in a small copper pot still. To create the secret recipe, the distillers were inspired by the herbs, spices, and botanicals in Anchor Brewing's very own Christmas Ale.

The taste This flavor-forward gin is light, crisp, and clean and combines a deep spiciness with subtle delicacy.

HOW TO ENJOY
Try it in a simple cocktail, such as a Gimlet.

Langley's No. 8

Gin, 41.7% ABV

DISTILLERY Langley Distillery, West Midlands, England. Spirit launched in 2009.
PHILOSOPHY The largest family-owned independent distillery in the UK, Langley uses only traditional methods.

The spirit English wheat grain spirit, water, and botanicals undergo a single distillation in Connie (a 660-gallon/3,000-liter pot still named after the Master Distiller's late mother).

The taste This kicks off with notes of juniper and coriander, which are followed by a fresh and grassy finish featuring pine notes and a balancing licorice sweetness.

HOW TO ENJOY
This is delicious mixed with top-quality tonic.

Loyalist

Gin, 40% ABV

DISTILLERY Sixty-six Gilead Distillery, Ontario, Canada. Founded in 2010.

PHILOSOPHY On an 80-acre (33-hectare) rural farm, this distillery uses highly detailed traditional techniques and state-of-the-art equipment.

The spirit In London Dry-style with no added sugar, this complex gin is made from locally harvested grains and hops, water sourced from limestone-filtered artesian wells, and a mix of locally sourced botanicals, including hand-picked juniper berries.

The taste Full-bodied and elegant, this gin gives off scents of flowers and lavender, with cucumber and licorice flavors on the palate.

This is a London Dry gin, so it is fitting that the Union Jack flag features on the label—a different version of the company's logo appears on each of its products

The name is inspired by the distillery's location in Prince Edward County, a United Empire Loyalist settlement in Ontario

SIXTY-SIX
gilead distillery

LOYALIST GIN

40% alc./vol. | 750ml
Product of/Produit du Canada

LETHERBEE ORIGINAL LABEL
LETHERBEE GIN
GIN FOR WELLNESS
1L (48% Alc. by Vol.)

Letherbee

Gin, 48% ABV

DISTILLERY Letherbee, Illinois, USA. Founded in 2011.

PHILOSOPHY Bartenders who make serious, cocktail-friendly spirits with bartenders in mind.

The spirit In a labor-intensive process, a base spirit is enhanced with a balanced blend of 11 botanicals—from coriander and cardamom to peppery cubeb berries. The gin is non-chill filtered so that robust botanicals can shine through.

The taste With a tangible mouthfeel, the spirit tastes of pepper and spice. A versatile and unique spirit that suits classic and craft cocktails.

McHenry Classic

Gin, 40% ABV

DISTILLERY McHenry Distillery, Tasmania, Australia. Founded in 2010.
PHILOSOPHY This family-run, environmentally sustainable distillery benefits from having five natural springs on site.

The spirit Lovingly handmade, McHenry's flagship gin is based on rigorous, old-fashioned, hands-on pot-distillation methods. Traditional botanicals are distilled in a Tasmanian-made 110-gallon (500-liter) pot still.

The taste Elegant and smooth, with a rich licorice flavor, the spirit gives off notes of all the classics: citrus peel, star anise, coriander, cardamom, orris root, and juniper.

Martin Miller's

Gin, 40% ABV

DISTILLERY Langley Distillery, West Midlands, England. Spirit launched in 1999.
PHILOSOPHY An innovative producer that brings the philosophy of tea-making to gin production.

The spirit The production team distills the dried peels of citrus fruits separately, away from earthy botanicals like juniper—this yields a more balanced, citrus-forward expression. The use of pure Icelandic spring water produces a soft mouthfeel, due to its purity and low mineral content.

The taste The strong citrus introduction gives way to juniper notes, followed by a lovely clean finish and a soft mouthfeel.

Monkey 47

Gin, 40% ABV

DISTILLERY Black Forest Distillers GmbH, Loßburg-Betzweiler, Germany. Founded in 2008.
PHILOSOPHY Inside a historic building that dates back to the mid-1700s, this modern distillery features a custom distillation plant, handmade by the region's famous coppersmiths.

The spirit The producer macerates 47 hand-picked ingredients in a mixture of pure molasses, alcohol, and soft spring water from the sandstone wells of the Black Forest. The spirit matures in traditional earthenware containers for at least three months, and is unfiltered in order to retain a full range of aromas.

The taste An invitingly sweet and flowery aroma with a hint of peppery spices gives way to crisp citrus notes. Notice the subtle bitter fruit notes of cranberries and lingonberries.

Notaris Jonge Graanjenever

Jenever, 35% ABV

DISTILLERY Herman Jansen Beverages, Schiedam, The Netherlands. Distillery founded in 1777.
PHILOSOPHY One of Holland's most lauded distilleries embraces family values, honesty, and hard work to create this jenever.

The spirit This 100 percent organic gin is made using grains sourced from the mill just behind the distillery, which are then combined with grain alcohol.

The taste A classic Dutch jenever, this sweet, grain-forward spirit offers notes of bread, yeast, and juniper.

No. 209

Gin, 46% ABV

DISTILLERY No. 209, California, USA. Spirit launched in 2005.
PHILOSOPHY Originally established in 1882 when it was the 209th permitted distillery in the United States, this innovative producer makes use of the best Old World distilling techniques.

The spirit The staff produces the gin using single-shot distillation in a copper alembic pot still. The base spirit is four-times column-distilled using Midwestern corn, and the water comes from snowmelt on the Sierra Nevada Mountains.

The taste No. 209 opens with a beautifully aromatic nose of citrus and floral notes. It features bergamot, coriander, and cassia flavor notes.

Pink Pepper (Audemus)

Gin, 44% ABV

PRODUCER Audemus Spirits, Cognac, France. Founded in 2013.
PHILOSOPHY Based in the heart of Cognac, Audemus draws inspiration from traditional distilling techniques, modern alchemy, and a passion for innovation.

The spirit This unusual gin is produced using reduced-pressure distillation—each aromatic macerates separately in alcohol and is then distilled. The team combines each extract with French wheat spirit, and the final product is non-chill filtered to retain an intense flavor and aroma.

The taste Fresh, spicy notes of pink pepper, juniper, and cardamom are prominent. Over time, the liquid evolves to produce notes of vanilla and honey.

Ransom Dry

Gin, 43% ABV

DISTILLERY Ransom Wine Co. & Distillery, Oregon, USA. Spirit launched in 2014.
PHILOSOPHY This versatile and award-winning distillery uses labor-intensive, traditional methods to produce spirits with great aromatic intensity and body.

The spirit This gin is made from a base ferment of malted barley and rye and an infusion of botanicals in corn-based spirit. Distillation occurs in a hand-hammered, direct-fired alembic pot still.

The taste Ethereal aromatics of hops and white flowers provide an inviting introduction, followed by a rich and silky liquid that is punctuated by citrus and exotic spices.

Portobello Road

Gin, 42% ABV

DISTILLERY Thames Distillers, London, England. Spirit launched in 2011.
PHILOSOPHY This forward-thinking producer is committed to exploring and celebrating the history of gin; the spirit was developed at The Ginstitute, one of London's smallest museums.

The spirit English-grown wheat forms the base spirit. The producer distills this with nine carefully selected botanical ingredients from around the world, including orris from Tuscany, juniper berries, Spanish lemon peels, and Indonesian nutmeg. The gin is bottled by hand.

The taste This versatile gin can work in a variety of cocktails. An initial burst of juniper gives way to a sustained citrus character, before closing with a warm peppery finish.

Rogue Society

Gin, 40% ABV

DISTILLERY Southern Grain Distillery, Canterbury, New Zealand. Spirit launched in 2014.
PHILOSOPHY From the bottom of the world comes a gin that benefits from more than three generations of experience.

The spirit In a historic nineteenth-century still, the team distills a clean neutral wheat spirit with glacial waters from the Southern Alps of New Zealand and 12 exotic botanicals sourced from around the world.

The taste Subtle floral hints of lavender and orange blossom give way to earthy tones of cinnamon bark and nutmeg, before vibrant citrus and juniper flavors coat the palate.

Sacred

Gin, 43.8% ABV

DISTILLERY Sacred Spirits, London, England. Founded in 2009.
PHILOSOPHY Using vacuum distillation to create truly original drinks of exceptional quality.

The spirit A total of 12 botanicals are used to make this gin—each of them is separately macerated and distilled with an English wheat base spirit to retain individual character and depth. The process allows no air contact, and takes at least four weeks.

The taste Almost creamy on the palate with a lush, juniper-led nose, this gin yields flavors of violet flowers, crushed cardamom pods, and cinnamon.

Sipsmith

Gin, 41.6% ABV

DISTILLERY The Sipsmith Distillery, London, England. Launched in 2009.
PHILOSOPHY Created to bring the lost art and craft of traditional copper distillation back to London, this distillery was the first of its kind to open in London for nearly 200 years.

The spirit Master Distiller Jared Brown is a world-renowned drink historian who trawled the history books for inspiration. The one-shot distillation process takes place in small batches to draw out all the impurities in the English wheat base.

The taste The quintessential expression of the London Dry style, this smooth, bold, and aromatic gin offers bright floral meadow aromas, followed by a growing citrus sweetness, and a hint of spice and violet on the finish.

Sloane's

Gin, 40% ABV

DISTILLERY Distilleries Group Toorank, Zevenaar, The Netherlands. Spirit launched in 2011.
PHILOSOPHY Using natural and unique ingredients in the distillation process to create balanced and smooth products.

The spirit Each of the nine botanicals are distilled individually, and then rested, before being blended to create an exceptionally smooth gin with an exquisite balance of flavors.

The taste This spirit is rich and full of flavor, with juniper definitely in charge. Citrus notes and a smooth finish complete the experience.

Spirit Works

Gin, 43% ABV

DISTILLERY Spirit Works Distillery, California, USA. Founded in 2012.

PHILOSOPHY Running a "grain-to-glass" distillery, the all-female production team mills, mashes, ferments, and distills organic whole grains on site.

The spirit After processing Red Winter wheat, the team applies a mix of eight Californian botanicals (juniper, coriander, cardamom, angelica root, orris root, hibiscus, and fresh zest from lemons and oranges) to the pot still.

The taste Wheat provides a round, slightly sweet base to this balanced gin. The botanicals contribute subtle spice and soft floral and fruit notes.

HOW TO ENJOY To savor the subtle notes, add just a splash of tonic.

Ungava

Gin, 43.1% ABV

DISTILLERY Domaine Pinnacle, Quebec, Canada. Spirit launched in 2010.

PHILOSOPHY This family-owned orchard and maple grove on mountain slopes began as a producer of ice cider and liqueurs. All products use natural and local Canadian ingredients.

The spirit Using a copper pot still and traditional techniques, this small-batch gin has a distinctive sunshine yellow color due to six rare botanicals—hand-picked in the wild during the summer—that are native to the Ungava region in Canada's Arctic tundra.

The taste Smooth, fresh, floral, and spicy, this unique spirit features the intriguing flavors of Nordic juniper, wild rose hips, cloudberry, crowberry, and arctic-blend and labrador teas.

V2C

Gin, 41.5% ABV

DISTILLERY Hoofvaartkerk Anno 1857, Hoofddorp, The Netherlands. Spirit launched in 2014.

PHILOSOPHY Once a hobby project, V2C is now a small but successful venture. The team focuses on quality, craftsmanship, natural resources, and a distinguished palate.

The spirit No additives, extracts, or filtering processes invade the small-batch process. The team sources the finest ingredients, such as juniper, angelica, orange, licorice, laurel, and St. John's Wort, from all over the world.

The taste This dry gin has a sophisticated full body. Every ingredient shines through—most especially coriander, cardamom, lemon, and ginger.

Williams GB

Gin, 40% ABV

DISTILLERY Chase Distillery, Herefordshire, England. Founded in 2008.
PHILOSOPHY This family-owned, single-estate distillery pays detailed attention to every stage of the production process. The producer fills and seals each bottle by hand.

The spirit Made from scratch using potatoes from the family farm, this gin is unlike many others (in which a neutral grain spirit is re-distilled with botanicals). The team use juniper buds and berries to ensure the driest results.

The taste Dry juniper jousts for attention with zesty citrus, followed by the warm and spicy notes of cinnamon, nutmeg, and ginger.

Victoria

Gin, 45% ABV

DISTILLERY Victoria Spirits, British Columbia, Canada. Founded in 2008.
PHILOSOPHY Situated on the idyllic Vancouver Island, this distillery makes premium spirits that are ideal for high-end, spirit-forward cocktails.

The spirit Each numbered, handmade batch of the distillery's flagship gin is produced in a German-made, 44-gallon (200-liter) pot still. The team bottle only the best-quality middle part of each run, known as the "heart."

The taste A smooth full-bodied spirit, this gin balances the characteristic evergreen flavor of juniper with notes of citrus, floral, and spice.

MORE to TRY

Botanica

Gin, 45% ABV

DISTILLERY Falcon Spirits Distillery, California, USA. Founded in 2012.
PHILOSOPHY Making innovative products using the best ingredients available, both locally and internationally.

This bold and well-rounded spirit is made using an intricate process. Flavor is preserved by separately distilling each botanical, such as citrus fruit. The team macerates, freezes, thaws, and vacuum-filters cucumbers. The gin tastes of bergamot, citrus, and cucumber, with a complex finish.

Jensen's Bermondsey

Gin, 43% ABV

DISTILLERY Bermondsey Distillery, London, England. Spirit launched in 2004.
PHILOSOPHY Taking inspiration from the delicate vintage gins of the twentieth century.

The staff add British wheat spirit, water, and classic botanicals to a John Dore still. The ingredients macerate for 9–15 hours (depending on the ambient temperature), then distillation begins. This smooth and well-balanced gin offers an inviting mouthfeel, with lightly floral aromas and a distinct lemon note on the palate.

Njord

Gin, 40% ABV

DISTILLERY Spirit of Njord, Mellerup, Denmark. Spirit launched in 2014.
PHILOSOPHY To develop Danish gin: small-batch and high-quality with a distinct flavor.

Using a German copper pot still, these makers ferment and distill over a two-month period using a one-shot method. Each batch is crafted, bottled, and labeled by hand. The smooth, complex, and balanced gin features notes of spruce, angelica, coriander, woodruff, and junipers.

Infusing Gin

The most botanical of all spirits, gin responds well to infusions. Note the flavors in gin that most appeal to you, and then infuse with those same flavors, or try new complementary ones. For best results, follow the instructions on pages 24–25.

Star Anise

A visually stunning infusion, star anise-flavored gin is perfect if you're a fan of pastis and licorice flavors.

What you need 1¾oz (50g) star anise; 3 cups gin.

Infusing time 2–3 days.

The next level Enhance the flavor by adding 1 tablespoon of whole cardamom pods to the mix.

Blueberry

Sweeten your gin by infusing it with cooked blueberries.

What you need 3½oz (100g) blueberries, cooked over low heat for a few minutes until they release juice; 3 cups gin.

Infusing time 1–2 weeks.

The next level Play around with fresh mint or citrus to offset the sweetness of the berries. If you can find tart sloe berries, simply apply those to this recipe to make your own sloe gin.

Lemongrass

Use sweet and floral lemongrass to complement any gin's botanical flavors.

What you need 2–3 lemongrass stalks, cut into chunks; 3 cups gin.

Infusing time 3–5 days.

The next level Toss in a few sprigs of fresh mint to make the infusion crisp and refreshing.

Lavender

For an extra-floral and aromatic expression, infuse gin with lavender.

What you need 1½ tsp dried culinary lavender; 3 cups gin.

Infusing time 1–2 days.

The next level Adding the peel of one lemon (pith removed) can temper the floral notes.

Grapefruit

Fresh grapefruit adds a pleasingly tart note to any gin.

What you need 1 medium grapefruit, peeled and cut into chunks; 3 cups gin.

Infusing time 3–5 days.

The next level Up the citrus notes by adding the peel of one lime (pith removed). A small chunk of fresh lemongrass gives a more complex result.

Rosemary

Fresh rosemary helps to heighten the savory elements in your gin.

What you need 2–3 sprigs of rosemary; 3 cups gin.

Infusing time 3–5 days.

The next level Add a small sliced cucumber to produce a gin that works beautifully with tonic.

Martini

The Martini is a grown-up cocktail from the late-nineteenth century that allows gin and vermouth to shine. Everyone agrees on the core ingredients, but an age-old debate persists—is it best shaken or stirred? Experts advocate stirring to prevent bubbles or ice shards. Make a classic, or create your own version—there are now hundreds of "-tinis" to try.

The Classic Recipe

Although the ratio of gin to vermouth varies from bartender to bartender, the classic Martini is always heavy on the spirits, so for best results you must serve it cold.

1 Pour 2½fl oz (75ml) dry gin into a shaker.

2 Add 1 tablespoon dry vermouth, fill with ice cubes, and stir until the mixture is cold.

3 Add 1 dash orange bitters. Stir again and strain into a chilled Martini glass.

Serve it up Garnish with an olive or lemon twist.

Create Your Own Signature Mix

Key Components

1 Pour **2½fl oz (75ml) dry gin** into a shaker.

Aficionados prefer a London-style dry gin (at a high proof), but try a light variety for a smoother taste. Swap out gin for vodka, and you may discover a cleaner, neutral flavor.

2 Add **1 tablespoon dry vermouth**, fill with **ice cubes**, and stir until the mixture is cold.

For a Perfect Martini, swap dry vermouth for equal parts sweet and dry. For a Bone Dry Martini, omit the vermouth, or replace it with a vermouth-rinse or -soaked toothpick to create a Desert Martini.

3 Add **1 dash orange bitters**. Stir again and strain into a chilled Martini glass.

Some recipes omit bitters completely, but they add to the flavor profile. Customize your Martini with a cutting-edge flavor, such as olive bitters.

Orange bitters

Vermouth

Gin

Additional Flourishes

Garnish As well as a lemon twist or olive, you could use a cocktail onion as a garnish (making a Gibson Martini). Make yours a Dirty Martini by adding a few extra olives and a splash of olive brine.

Skewers Make tomato, olive, and mozzarella skewers, or wrap thin slices of cucumber into a "rose" and secure with a skewer.

Craft Reinventions

The only rule in the Martini game is that there are no rules. Purists scoff, but bartenders take great liberties with the drink—and the possibilities are endless. Try variations that push boundaries but remain true to the soul of the original.

Spicy Heirloom Tomato Martini

Mix the gin, tomato juice, pickle juice, and horseradish in a shaker. Fill with ice cubes, stir until cold, and strain into a chilled Martini glass. Garnish with the chive blossoms. Serve.

- 3 chive blossoms
- dash of freshly grated horseradish
- 1½ tsp pickle juice
- 1fl oz (30ml) heirloom tomato juice
- 3fl oz (90ml) gin

Espresso Martini

Mix the vodka, espresso, and liqueur in a shaker. Fill with ice cubes, stir until cold, and strain into a chilled Martini glass. Top with the coffee beans, and serve.

- chocolate-covered coffee beans
- 1fl oz (30ml) coffee liqueur
- 1fl oz (30ml) cold espresso
- 2fl oz (60ml) vodka

◀ Cucumber Saketini

Mix the vodka, sake, and cucumber juice in a shaker. Fill with crushed ice, shake for 15 seconds, and strain into a chilled Martini glass. Thread a thin cucumber slice on a skewer, and serve.

- Japanese cucumber slice
- 1 tbsp cucumber juice
- 2½fl oz (75ml) dry sake
- 1fl oz (30ml) vodka

French 75

The French 75 is the world's favorite Champagne cocktail. It can be traced back to 1915, at the New York Bar in Paris—later known as Harry's New York. Bar staff compared the cocktail's kick to that of the powerful French 75mm howitzer gun, and the French 75 was born. Perfect your own version of this simple and elegant cocktail.

The Classic Recipe

The French 75 brings out the best in simple and straightforward flavors and the finest ingredients.

1 Pour 1fl oz (30ml) dry gin into a shaker.

2 Add 1 tablespoon lemon juice.

3 Add 1 tablespoon simple syrup. Fill the shaker with ice cubes and shake vigorously for 10 seconds.

4 Strain into an iced Champagne flute. Fill to the top with brut Champagne.

Serve it up Garnish with a long lemon twist.

Create Your Own Signature Mix

Key Components

1 Pour **1fl oz (30ml) gin** into a shaker.

For a stronger drink, double the volume of gin. You could try a complex gin instead of a dry one. If you like sweet flavors, add a dash of brandy or Cointreau.

2 Add **1 tablespoon fresh lemon juice**.

. Using fresh lemon juice is always best, but you could also try fresh lime or grapefruit juice.

3 Add **1 tablespoon simple syrup**. Fill the shaker with **ice cubes** and shake vigorously for 10 seconds.

Simple syrup blends better than sugar alternatives, but mix things up with agave syrup instead.

4 Strain into an iced Champagne flute. Fill to the top with **brut Champagne**.

There is no need to use high-end Champagne—standard Champagne works very well. For a sweeter option, use rosé Champagne or Prosecco.

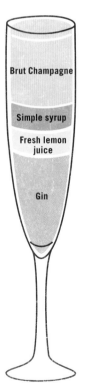

Brut Champagne

Simple syrup

Fresh lemon juice

Gin

Additional Flourishes

Garnish Add a touch of jazz with a garnish of candied lemon peel or a slice of ginger.

Fruit Why not drop a raspberry or blueberry into the glass before you pour? Don't forget to eat it afterward—it will taste boozy and delicious.

Flowers Add a lightly floral note with some lavender-infused simple syrup, or a dash of pear or elderflower bitters.

Craft Reinventions

Bartenders play around with a variety of fresh fruits and fruity liqueurs that complement Champagne, or experiment with different kinds of bubbles. Such experiments produced these three innovative recipes on the right.

Pear 75

Pour the pear brandy and syrup into a mixing glass. Add ice cubes and stir until cold. Strain into a flute, then top up with Champagne. Garnish with the lemon twist, and serve.

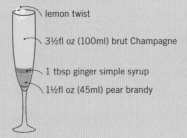

lemon twist

3½fl oz (100ml) brut Champagne

1 tbsp ginger simple syrup

1½fl oz (45ml) pear brandy

Blood Orange 75

Pour the gin, juice, syrup, and bitters into a mixing glass. Add ice cubes and stir until cold. Strain into a flute, then top up with Champagne. Garnish with the twist, and serve.

blood orange twist

3½fl oz (100ml) brut Champagne

dash of orange bitters

1½ tsp simple syrup

1 tbsp fresh blood orange juice

1½fl oz (45ml) gin

◀ Rosé 75

Pour the gin, juice, and syrup into a mixing glass. Add ice cubes and stir until cold. Strain into a flute, then top up with rosé Champagne. Garnish with crystallized rose petals. Serve.

crystallized rose petals

3½fl oz (100ml) rosé Champagne

1½ tsp simple syrup

1 tbsp fresh lemon juice

1oz (30ml) gin

Gimlet

The Gimlet is the perfect mix of lime juice and gin, and a staple on any classic cocktail menu. You can trace the drink back to the nineteenth century, when sailors mixed it with Rose's lime cordial to make a medicinal tonic. If you're just beginning to mix craft cocktails, start with the Gimlet—it is the perfect platform for many new varieties.

The Classic Recipe

Start off with your favorite gin, grab some fresh lime juice, and you have everything you need for a tart classic Gimlet.

1 Pour 2½fl oz (75ml) gin into a shaker.
2 Add 1 tablespoon fresh lime juice. Fill the shaker with ice cubes and shake for 10 seconds. Strain into a chilled coupe glass.
Serve it up Garnish with a lime wheel.

Create Your Own Signature Mix

Key Components

1 Pour **2½fl oz (75ml) gin** into a shaker.

To best enjoy the tartness of lime, opt for a clean and neutral-tasting gin. For a complex Gimlet, play with flavor-rich craft varieties. Replace gin with vodka for a smooth-tasting Gimlet.

2 Add **1 tablespoon fresh lime juice**. Fill the shaker with **ice cubes** and shake for 10 seconds. Strain into your chilled glass.

Freshly squeezed lime juice lends a tart note; if you seek more sweetness, add simple syrup and reduce the volume of lime.

Fresh lime juice

Gin

Additional Flourishes

Garnish A lime wheel is the most common garnish, but you may find a crisp cucumber slice works just as well.

Herbs If you feel like breaking the rules, decorate with a fresh herb (such as thyme or basil) that complements your gin selection.

Berries Tart blueberries and raspberries offer a new flavor dimension—muddle them with lime juice or add them whole.

Craft Reinventions

A Gimlet is not a Gimlet without a tart citrus note, but bartenders far and wide have been playing around with fresh herbs and alternatives to lime. The variation recipes on the right can help you develop a taste for the unexpected.

Basil Gimlet

Muddle the basil leaves, lime juice, and syrup in a shaker. Add the gin, fill with ice cubes, shake for 10 seconds, and strain into a chilled coupe. Garnish with a basil leaf, and serve.

- basil leaf
- 1½fl oz (45ml) gin
- 1 tbsp simple syrup
- ¾fl oz (20ml) fresh lime juice
- handful of basil leaves

Cucumber Mint Gimlet

Muddle the mint leaves, lime juice, cucumber, and syrup in a shaker. Add the gin, fill with ice cubes, shake for 10 seconds, and strain into a chilled coupe. Top with cucumber, and serve.

- slice of cucumber
- 1½fl oz (45ml) gin
- 1 tbsp simple syrup
- 5 slices of cucumber
- ¾fl oz (20ml) fresh lime juice
- handful of mint leaves

◀ Grapefruit Vodka Gimlet

Combine the vodka, grapefruit juice, and agave syrup in a shaker. Fill with ice cubes, shake for 10 seconds, and pour into a chilled coupe. Garnish with grapefruit peel, and serve.

- sliced grapefruit peel
- 1 tbsp agave syrup
- ¾fl oz (20ml) fresh grapefruit juice
- 2fl oz (60ml) vodka

Gin Fizz

The Gin Fizz is the best-known member of the "Fizz" family of cocktails. It was first listed in the cocktail guides of the late nineteenth century. The drink became one of America's most popular choices, forcing bars to employ teams of bartenders to take turns using their muscle to create frothy perfection. Find out how to shake your way to a perfect "Fizz."

The Classic Recipe

This classic gets its trademark froth with an extra-firm shake.

1 Pour 2fl oz (60ml) dry gin into a shaker.

2 Add 1fl oz (30ml) fresh lemon juice.

3 Add 1fl oz (30ml) simple syrup. Fill with ice cubes and shake vigorously for 10 seconds.

4 Fill a collins glass with ice cubes. Strain the mixture from the shaker into the glass.

5 Top with soda, stir, and serve.

Create Your Own Signature Mix

Key Components

1 Pour **2fl oz (60ml) dry gin** into a shaker.

The classic uses a dry gin. For a more complex flavor, replace with a botanical variety.

2 Add **1fl oz (30ml) fresh lemon juice**.

For a more enhanced flavor, swap in mellow and sweet Meyer lemon juice instead.

3 Add **1fl oz (30ml) simple syrup**. Fill with ice cubes and shake vigorously.

When making simple syrup (see p27), add an additional citrus peel or fresh mint to complement the flavors.

4 Fill a collins glass with **ice cubes**. Strain the mixture from the shaker into the glass.

Replace plain ice with flavored ice cubes—add lemon juice or chopped cilantro to the water before freezing.

5 Top with **soda**, stir, and serve.

You could use more bubbles or shake the cocktail for longer for extra fizz. Try lemon-flavored soda, or sparkling wine (known as a Diamond Fizz).

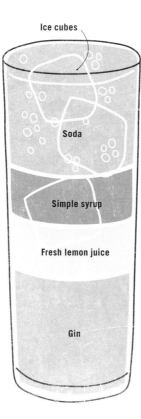

Ice cubes

Soda

Simple syrup

Fresh lemon juice

Gin

Additional Flourishes

Garnish Try ingredients that pair well with gin, such as cucumber, citrus, or fresh herbs.

Froth For a Silver Fizz, add an egg white to the other core ingredients and shake away, or use a whole egg (beaten first, then added to the shaker) to create a Golden Fizz.

Liqueurs Add 1 tablespoon of a liqueur, such as mint or melon, to turn a classic Gin Fizz on its head.

Craft Reinventions

Numerous Gin Fizz variations fill cocktail lists all over the world. Fresh eggs are used for extra froth and some mixologists add a colorful liqueur to give the drink more impact. Here are three of the best to try.

Mint Gin Fizz

Pour the gin, juice, liqueur, and syrup into a shaker. Add ice cubes, shake for 15 seconds, and strain into an ice-filled collins glass. Top up with soda, garnish with lemon and mint, and serve.

- slice of lemon and a mint sprig
- soda
- 1 tbsp simple syrup
- 1 tbsp mint liqueur
- 1 tbsp fresh lemon juice
- 2fl oz (60ml) gin

Whisky Fizz

Mix the whisky, juice, syrup, and egg white in a shaker. Shake for 10 seconds, add ice, and shake again. Strain into an ice-filled collins glass. Top up with soda and bitters, and add the cherry. Serve.

- maraschino cherry
- 2 dashes cherry bitters
- soda
- 1 egg white
- 1 tbsp simple syrup
- 1 tbsp fresh lemon juice
- 2fl oz (60ml) whisky

◀ Watermelon Gin Fizz

Pour the gin, juices, and syrup into a shaker. Add ice, shake for 15 seconds, and strain into an ice-filled collins glass. Fill to the top with soda, garnish with watermelon, and serve.

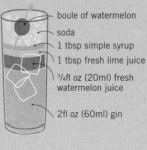

- boule of watermelon
- soda
- 1 tbsp simple syrup
- 1 tbsp fresh lime juice
- 3/4fl oz (20ml) fresh watermelon juice
- 2fl oz (60ml) gin

The Gin Sling dates to the late eighteenth century. It is often confused with the modern Singapore Sling, but an old-school Gin Sling features fruit brandy and is less sweet than its brilliant-red relative. The sophisticated cocktail is the perfect union of dry, sweet, and sour flavors, and a fantastic choice for new interpretations.

The Classic Recipe

A party favorite, the classic Gin Sling marries dry gin with a sweet vermouth.

1 Pour 1½fl oz (45ml) gin into a shaker.
2 Add 1fl oz (30ml) sweet vermouth.
3 Pour in ¾fl oz (20ml) fresh lemon juice.
4 Add 1fl oz (30ml) simple syrup.
5 Add 1 dash Angostura bitters. Shake for 10 seconds.
6 Fill a collins glass with ice cubes. Strain the mixture from the shaker into the glass.
7 Fill to the top with soda.
Serve it up Garnish with a lemon twist.

Create Your Own Signature Mix

Key Components

1 Pour **1½fl oz (45ml) gin** into a shaker.
Opt for a light and clean craft variety.

2 Add **1fl oz (30ml) sweet vermouth**.
Swap in Cointreau, grenadine, or grated nutmeg for sweet vermouth.

3 Pour in **¾fl oz (20ml) fresh lemon juice**.
For a tart flavor, opt for lime juice.

4 Add **1fl oz (30ml) simple syrup**.
Slings need a sweet touch—any mix of simple syrup, sugar, grenadine, or pineapple juice works.

5 Add **1 dash Angostura bitters**.
Shake for 10 seconds.
We live in a golden era of bitters—swap in a fun flavor to liven it up.

6 Fill your glass with **ice cubes**. Strain the mixture into the glass.
Use firm, large ice cubes so the drink remains cold.

7 Fill to the top with **soda**.
Soda adds sparkle, but you can replace it with fresh fruit juice.

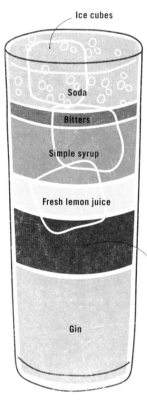

Ice cubes
Soda
Bitters
Simple syrup
Fresh lemon juice
Sweet vermouth
Gin

Additional Flourishes

Garnish Impart a bright, clean aroma with a lemon decoration—a twist of peel, wedge, or wheel all work perfectly.

Tartness Add tart fruit, such as sour cherries, to your glass to add oomph to a standard Gin Sling.

Craft Reinventions

Mixologists love to spruce up a standard Sling. Some add fruit liqueurs, and others enhance the tart flavors with different notes of citrus and bitters. These are three of the best variations around.

Aviation

Pour the gin, liqueurs, and juice into a shaker. Add ice cubes, shake for 10 seconds, and strain into a chilled collins glass. Top up with soda. Stir, garnish with the cherry, and serve.

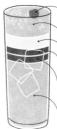

maraschino cherry

soda

1 tbsp fresh lemon juice

1½ tsp crème de violette (violet liqueur)

1½ tsp maraschino liqueur

2fl oz (60ml) gin

Oahu Gin Sling

Pour the gin, juice, liqueurs, and syrup into a shaker. Add ice, shake for 10 seconds, and strain into an ice-filled collins glass. Top up with soda, and stir. Garnish with the twist, and serve.

lime twist

soda

¾ tsp simple syrup

1 tbsp Bénédictine herbal liqueur

1 tbsp crème de cassis

1fl oz (30ml) fresh lime juice

2fl oz (60ml) gin

◀ Pomegranate Gin Sling

Pour the gin, juice, and syrup into a shaker. Add ice, shake for 10 seconds, and strain into an ice-filled collins glass. Top up with soda, garnish with the pomegranate and lime, and serve.

lime wheel and pomegranate seeds

soda

1½ tsp simple syrup

1fl oz (30ml) fresh pomegranate juice

2fl oz (60ml) gin

Whisky begins life as grains that are processed into a beer-like "wort" and distilled into a spirit. To finish, the spirit is aged in wooden barrels. A **host of variables**—from the location, grains, and barrels, to the **distillation method**—dictate whether it becomes a Scotch, single or blended malt, bourbon, rye, or blend. Many distilleries have **specialized** their craft by focusing on a particular style, while others produce a wider range of whiskies and **experiment** with aged varieties that won't see the light of day until years have passed. Whisky is **strong and expressive** at its core, but many of the fine whiskies in this chapter are blended and aged to give rise to **soft, subtle notes** of flavor. Delve into the world of whisky in this chapter and create complementary infusions and modern cocktails that **bring out the best** in the spirit.

WHISKY, BOURBON, AND RYE

1792 Small Batch

Bourbon whiskey, 46.85% ABV

DISTILLERY Barton 1792 Distillery, Kentucky, USA. Founded in 1879.
PHILOSOPHY The oldest fully operating distillery in Kentucky—the "Bourbon Capital of the World"—has transformed traditional distilling.

The spirit The distillery's signature "high rye" bourbon recipe imparts this spirit with spicy notes of rye. To achieve the finished result, the Master Distiller carefully blends select barrels in small batches.

The taste Expressive and elegant, this bourbon finds balance from fleeting flavors of sweet caramel and vanilla.

Asheville Blonde

Whiskey, 40% ABV

DISTILLERY Asheville Distilling Company, North Carolina, USA. Founded in 2010.
PHILOSOPHY A true "plow-to-pour" distillery, this producer grows its own heirloom grains and distills them with others from the local area.

The spirit This heirloom-grain whiskey is created with fermented white corn and extremely rare "turkey red" wheat. The producer distills the mash in a 1,100 gallon (5,000-liter) German pot still with two columns. The spirit is aged in charred white oak barrels.

The taste This smooth spirit features hints of vanilla, buttered popcorn, tobacco, cherry, and chocolate.

Bain's Cape Mountain

Whisky, 43% ABV

DISTILLERY James Sedgwick Distillery, Western Cape, South Africa. Founded in 2003.
PHILOSOPHY Inspired by the Cape Mountains, this producer creates the only whisky that is made entirely from South African maize.

The spirit The team processes the finest South African grain, then distills it in column stills. The whisky is aged for three years in medium-charred American used bourbon oak barrels, and is then matured in a fresh batch of similar barrels for 18–30 months.

The taste Smooth and warm, this spirit has notes of oak, vanilla, and cocoa butter, with a long and spicy finish.

Corsair Triple Smoke

Whiskey, 40% ABV

DISTILLERY Corsair Artisan Distillery, Tennessee, USA. Founded in 2008.
PHILOSOPHY One of America's most innovative producers, Corsair creates new styles of spirits.

The spirit This complex whiskey is made in small 700-gallon (3,200-liter) batches using cherry wood-smoked, peat-smoked, and beechwood-smoked malts. The producers distill in a 250-gallon (1,100-liter) antique copper pot still.

The taste The three types of malt impart strong and sweet yet smoky notes on the nose, palate, and finish.

Blanton's Single Barrel

Bourbon whiskey, 46.5% ABV

DISTILLERY Buffalo Trace Distillery, Kentucky, USA. Spirit launched in 1984.
PHILOSOPHY Harnessing inspiration from Colonel Albert Blanton, who was a leading pioneer in the development of bourbon.

The spirit Taken from the center-cut—or middle sections—of the distillery's famous Warehouse H, this bourbon is made of corn, rye, and malted barley. It was the first single-barrel bourbon.

The taste Spicy aromas of dried citrus, caramel, and vanilla delight the nose, while the soft liquid gives off flavors of burnt sugar, orange, and cloves.

Dad's Hat

Rye whiskey, 45% ABV

DISTILLERY Mountain Laurel Spirits, Pennsylvania, USA. Founded in 2011.
PHILOSOPHY In the birthplace of rye whiskey, this producer uses only natural, local ingredients and the most careful methods to honor the spirit's roots.

The spirit Distilled in the traditional Pennsylvania style, this spirit features a high malt content, without any corn. Double-distilled in a 440-gallon (2,000-liter) pot still, the spirit is aged in 15-gallon (70-liter) new American white oak barrels for an average of eight and a half months.

The taste This spicy, well-balanced rye reveals a malty sweetness over time. Sharp pepper, caraway, and fresh cinnamon give way to undertones of cocoa and dried fruit.

Dillon's White

Rye whiskey, 40% ABV

DISTILLERY Dillon's Small Batch Distillers, Ontario, Canada. Founded in 2012.
PHILOSOPHY Committed to highlighting the use of fresh and local ingredients.

The spirit The distillery works with a local malter and miller to create a rye that is crafted from 100 percent Ontario rye grain, yeast, and water. Once the grain has been mashed and fermented, it is distilled twice through two separate pot stills.

The taste Raw and smooth, with only a fleeting hint of sweetness, this spicy rye reveals the complexity of the grain.

Dalmore King Alexander III

Scotch whisky, 40% ABV

DISTILLERY The Dalmore Distillery, Alness, Scotland. Founded in 1839.
PHILOSOPHY This producer has stayed true to its history by defying aging convention and creating bold and adventurous single malt whiskies.

The spirit This whisky is the only single malt in the world to be finished in six kinds of barrels—from bourbon and sherry to port and wine—all of which are hand selected by the Master Distiller, Richard Paterson.

The taste Red berry fruits and fresh flowers delight the nose, while the palate responds to notes of citrus zest, vanilla, crème caramel, cinnamon, and nutmeg.

Dillon's lists how each spirit is made and what it is made of on each of their bottles

Hand-written numbers signify each batch

Excelsior

Bourbon whiskey, 48% ABV

DISTILLERY Coppersea Distilling, New York, USA. Founded in 2011.
PHILOSOPHY This farm distillery produces "the first 100 percent New York bourbon," using local grains and barrels from New York.

The spirit Local grains—corn, rye, and barley—ferment in open-top wooden tanks and form the foundation of this spirit, which is distilled twice and barrel-aged in barrels that are made in New York.

The taste This high-rye bourbon has peppery notes that counterbalance the sweetness of the corn. The barrels impart notes of vanilla, cedar, and fir.

Eagle Rare

Bourbon whiskey, 45% ABV

DISTILLERY Buffalo Trace Distillery, Kentucky, USA. Spirit launched in 1975.
PHILOSOPHY One of Kentucky's most famous and historic distilleries produces a complex bourbon with unique characteristics.

The spirit Masterfully crafted and carefully aged for no less than ten years, every barrel of this straight bourbon whiskey is carefully selected to offer consistent flavor but with an individual personality.

The taste The complex nose includes hints of herbs, honey, leather, and oak. Notes of candied almonds and cocoa delight the palate, followed by a dry, lingering finish.

Few

Bourbon whiskey, 46.5% ABV

DISTILLERY Few Spirits, Illinois, USA. Founded in 2011.
PHILOSOPHY This is a true "grain-to-glass" distillery—the staff ferments local grain, then distills, ages, and bottles everything in house.

The spirit The producer sources the finest grain possible and mashes it, before putting it through temperature-controlled fermentation to become a wash. The wash is distilled, finished, and rested in new American oak barrels.

The taste This sweet and spicy bourbon packs in notes of cinnamon and clove, with a peppery bite on the finish.

Glendalough Double Barrel

Irish whiskey, 42% ABV

DISTILLERY Glendalough Distillery, County Wicklow, Ireland. Spirit launched in 2014.
PHILOSOPHY As Ireland's first modern craft distillery, this producer aims to recapture Ireland's lost heritage of great spirit production and create new and exciting contemporary spirits.

The spirit Distilled in a column still in small batches, this single-grain Irish whiskey is made from locally sourced malted barley and corn. It is then aged for three and a half years in used bourbon oak barrels, then finally in a sherry barrel for six months.

The taste Cherry, raisin, and fig delight the nose, and the palate revels in notes of butterscotch, honey, dried fruit, and peppercorn.

Double Barrel won Double Gold at the International Wine and Spirits Competition 2015 in San Francisco

In sixth-century Ireland, monks, such as Saint Kevin (featured here) were the first to distill alcohol for consumption

Garrison Brothers Cowboy

Bourbon whiskey, 68% ABV

DISTILLERY Garrison Brothers Distillery, Texas, USA. Founded in 2006.
PHILOSOPHY To build and sustain a family-owned distillery—the first legal whiskey distillery in Texas—and produce spirits of the highest quality.

The spirit This producer ferments a sweet mash composed of organic, non-GMO corn, wheat, and malted barley for five days, and then distills it in three custom-made copper pot stills. It ages for three years in custom-made, charred white American oak barrels.

The taste A pleasant mouthfeel opens out to traces of wood, caramel, coconut, pecan, cornmeal, and cinnamon.

Hillrock Solera Aged

Bourbon whiskey, 46.3% ABV

DISTILLERY Hillrock Estate Distillery, New York, USA. Founded in 2010.
PHILOSOPHY This distillery is the first in the US since pre-Prohibition to handcraft whiskey on site from estate-grown grain. It embodies the rich distilling history of New York's Hudson Valley.

The spirit The producers plant and harvest heirloom grains (barley, corn, and rye), and distill the ferment in small batches using a 250-gallon (1,100-liter) copper pot still. Finally, they age the spirit using a blending method known as Solera.

The taste The golden amber liquid smells of caramel and vanilla, with floral and fruity notes. The palate picks up flavors that range from maple syrup and rock candy, to clove and cinnamon.

High West Silver

Whiskey, 40% ABV

DISTILLERY High West Distillery, Utah, USA. Founded in 2007.
PHILOSOPHY This scenic distillery uses exact science and the best ingredients to distill elegance from the grain.

The spirit Produced in small batches in a traditional copper pot still from plump western oats, this spirit spends only five minutes in toasted oak barrels to minimize their influence on the flavor.

The taste Slightly sweet elements battle for attention with more aggressive, somewhat sour, notes. Cocoa and coconut flavors give way to a smooth, vanilla finish.

Hudson Baby

Bourbon whiskey, 46% ABV

DISTILLERY Tuthilltown Spirits, New York, USA. Founded in 2003.
PHILOSOPHY The first distillery to open and produce whiskey in New York State since Prohibition, Tuthilltown uses exclusively locally grown grains.

The spirit Local grains are fermented, and two distillations occur; the first distillation includes the whole mash. Aging takes place in new, charred American white oak barrels.

The taste This approachable bourbon provides an ideal introduction to the spirit for the novice bourbon drinker. Mildly sweet, with a long finish.

Hudson Baby Bourbon

Hudson Baby Bourbon is the flagship spirit from the pioneering Tuthilltown Spirits distillery. It was the first whiskey to be made in New York State since Prohibition, and the first bourbon ever to be made in the state. The distillery has grown in prestige in recent years, but it still retains its small-batch, artisanal distilling process.

What's the story?

Tuthilltown Spirits uses a small-batch, "grain-to-glass" approach—just as it did when it started in 2005. To make Hudson Baby Bourbon, the team starts with a mash of local heirloom variety grains—95 percent corn and 5 percent barley—sourced from within 40 miles (64 kilometers) of the distillery. They distill the mash in four German-made pot stills, and then age the spirit in two different kinds of white oak charred barrels—their signature "baby" microcasks, and larger barrels—for one to three years to impart a rich, full flavor. The whiskey is then blended to achieve a balanced flavor profile. Every bottle is sealed with wax and numbered by hand.

More recently, the distillery's line has expanded to include Manhattan Rye, Four Grain Bourbon, and Single Malt.

What's next?

Tuthilltown are working on seasonal limited editions, such as Hudson Maple Cask Rye—the result of a cask-exchange programme with a local artisanal maple-syrup tapper.

The distillery is focused on the future of craft distilling. Recognized by *Spirits Business Magazine* as one of the Top 10 Most Pioneering Distillers of 2014, Erenzo continues to represent independent distillers as a board member of the American Craft Spirits Association, sharing the benefit of his experience and success.

Right Erenzo looks on as a staff member monitors the distilling process at Tuthilltown Spirits in Gardiner, New York.

Who is behind it?

Ralph Erenzo, self-taught distiller and founder of Hudson, hadn't set out to make spirits at first, but inspired by the historic Grist Mill on his property, his mind turned to whiskey. After two years of experimentation, Erenzo and his distilling partner, Brian Lee, produced their first batch, and one year later Hudson Baby Bourbon went on sale. A leader of the craft distilling movement, Ralph lobbied to remove red tape and kick-start craft spirits in New York.

Erenzo lobbies on the US **national stage** to support the industry **he loves**

First spirit produced in
2005

2010 American
Artisan Distillery
of the Year
(American Distilling Institute)

2011 American Craft
Whiskey Distillery of
the Year *(Whisky Magazine)*

2011
Artisan Whiskey
of the Year
(Whisky Guild)

Above Every bottle of Hudson whiskey is
individually sealed and numbered by hand.

Ichiro's Malt

Whisky, 46% ABV

DISTILLERY Chichibu Distillery, Saitama, Japan. Founded in 2008.
PHILOSOPHY Founded by whisky-lovers, this is one of Japan's most acclaimed whisky producers—seeking out innovative practices while maintaining traditional procedures.

The spirit A small distillery produces this rare and highly sought-after malt whisky in small quantities. The producer applies an intricate craftsmanship to the production process, with barrel-making and repairs being undertaken on site.

The taste This dark spirit has sweet peat on the nose, with smoky notes. The palate picks up flavors of wood and vanilla.

Journeyman W.R.

Rye whiskey, 45% ABV

DISTILLERY Journeyman Distillery, Michigan, USA. Founded in 2011.
PHILOSOPHY This thoughtful producer is committed to a handcrafted approach, using facilities that are steeped in family history.

The spirit The production team distills locally sourced rye, wheat, and a touch of barley in a copper pot still. The finished spirit spends less than 24 hours in new white American oak barrels before being cut to proof and bottled.

The taste The nose includes essences of raisin bread, fruit cake, and flowers, and the dry-yet-fruity body carries notes of vanilla, oatmeal, and peppery spice.

Juuri

Rye whisky, 46.3% ABV

DISTILLERY Kyrö Distillery, Isokyrö, Finland. Spirit launched in 2014.
PHILOSOPHY Kyrö's motto is "In Rye We Trust"— they use the grain in all of their spirits.

The spirit This unaged rye undergoes a long fermentation time to pack the spirit with flavor. All the brewing tanks are temperature-controlled to avoid lactic acids. Aging occurs in new American white oak barrels.

The taste Elements of fresh rye bread dominate the experience, although sweet notes of berries and dried plum also shine through.

Kavalan Classic Single Malt

Whisky, 40% ABV

DISTILLERY Kavalan Distillery, Yuan-Shan, Taiwan. Founded in 1996.
PHILOSOPHY Given its challenging, sub-tropical climate, this distillery thrives in the maturation process—the Master Blender tastes the whiskies on a daily basis.

The spirit Made with local mountain water and malted barley (mainly from Europe), the spirit is double-distilled in four pot stills. After aging in oak barrels, different varieties are blended.

The taste Fresh, clean, and rich, this whisky is full of sub-tropical fruit flavors such as mango, green apple, and cherry.

"Komagatake" The Revival

Whisky, 59% ABV

DISTILLERY Shinshu Mars Distillery, Nagano, Japan. Founded in 1984.
PHILOSOPHY This producer adheres to the highest standards to craft an exceptional whisky.

The spirit This producer uses water from Japan's Central Alps to create this flavor-rich spirit. Filtered once through decomposed granite soil, the liquid is matured in bourbon barrels that help to impart a light amber color.

The taste This balanced expression includes hints of fruit and peat. The palate instantly responds to fresh malt flavors.

Kopper Kettle

Whiskey, 43% ABV

DISTILLERY Belmont Farm Distillery, Virginia, USA. Founded in 1987.
PHILOSOPHY This farm-based distillery uses grains grown on site to produce a truly "grain-to-glass" spirit.

The spirit Once distilled, the whiskey is then charcoal-filtered and presoaked with oak and apple wood chips, which impart a distinct flavor. The whiskey is aged in oak barrels for four years.

The taste A softly spicy nose gives way to sweet tastes of vanilla and caramel apple. The warm, pleasant finish lacks any burn.

Koval Single Barrel

Bourbon whiskey, 47% ABV

DISTILLERY Koval Distillery, Illinois, USA. Founded in 2008.

PHILOSOPHY The owners of this—the first distillery to open in Chicago since the mid-1800s—left their academic careers to devote themselves to making organic spirits from scratch.

The spirit A mash bill of 51 percent corn and 49 percent millet—both milled on site—is processed and then barrel-aged for two to four years in white American oak barrels.

The taste Notes of mango, vanilla, caramel, and spice jostle for attention, with a forceful finish.

Lark Single Malt

Whisky, 43% ABV

DISTILLERY Lark Distillery, Tasmania, Australia. Founded in 1992.

PHILOSOPHY This producer creates quality single malt whisky using only the best Tasmanian ingredients.

The spirit Local malted barley, 50 percent of which is smoked with peat, is processed with mountain water, and left to ferment for a very long time—seven days. The spirit is double-distilled and matured for five to eight years in French and American oak barrels.

The taste This spirit achieves a balance between floral and fruit notes and heavy, earthy flavors on the finish.

Low Gap 2 Year Wheat

Whiskey, 43.1% ABV

DISTILLERY American Craft Whiskey Distillery, California, USA. Founded in 2008.

PHILOSOPHY Blazing new trails by distilling premium spirits in an antique Cognac still.

The spirit Double-distilled by hand in an antique 350-gallon (1,600-liter) Cognac still, this smooth whiskey is made from malted Bavarian hard wheat, and cut to proof with filtered rainwater.

The taste This subtly complex, full-flavored, and fruity whiskey has superb length and a grain-laced finish. It drinks almost like an aromatic brandy.

McKenzie

Rye whiskey, 45.5% ABV

DISTILLERY Finger Lakes Distilling, New York, USA. Founded in 2008.
PHILOSOPHY Taking an old-fashioned approach to distilling, from using locally sourced ingredients to open-top fermentations.

The spirit Over 90 percent of the spirit's raw materials come from within an 50-mile (80-km) radius of the distillery. Once fermentation is complete, the mash runs through an 25-foot (8.5-meter) continuous column still at a low proof to preserve flavor, and is then aged in new American white oak barrels and used sherry barrels.

The taste This spirit's bold rye flavor is complemented by bright notes of spice, dried fruit, and orange.

Mackmyra Svensk Ek

Whisky, 46.1% ABV

DISTILLERY Mackmyra, Norrland, Sweden. Founded in 1999.
PHILOSOPHY This eco-friendly producer uses local ingredients in all elements of the production process.

The spirit Using a 115-foot (35-meter) tall facility, the distilling process runs smoothly from the top, where crushed Swedish barley is added, to the bottom, where the finished spirit is ready to be aged in oak barrels.

The taste This whisky offers notes of sandalwood, dried ginger, black pepper, roasted oak barrel, and herbs, with a light, sweet oakiness on the finish.

Monkey Shoulder

Scotch whisky, 40% ABV

PRODUCER Monkey Shoulder, Dufftown, Scotland. Founded in 2005.
PHILOSOPHY Aiming to balance the complexity of a single malt with the accessibility of a blended Scotch.

The spirit A first-of-its-kind blend of three Speyside single malts, this spirit is matured in bourbon barrels. The Malt Master hand-selects the malts, and then blends them together in a small marrying tun for three to six months.

The taste Sweet, rich vanilla flavors, along with zesty notes of orange and ginger, are balanced with oak and a hint of spice.

Old Potrero

Rye whiskey, 48.5% ABV

DISTILLERY Anchor Brewing & Distilling Company, California, USA. Founded in 1993.
PHILOSOPHY These innovators helped to spark the modern craft spirits movement in San Francisco and beyond.

The spirit One of America's most decorated breweries, Anchor now uses small copper pot stills to create an expressive rye whiskey from a mash of 100 percent malted rye. The spirit is aged in handmade, charred oak barrels.

The taste This expressive spirit sports a rich color and unique character, with the distinctive taste of rye grain shining through.

Ranger Creek .36

Bourbon whiskey, 48% ABV

DISTILLERY Ranger Creek Brewing and Distilling, Texas, USA. Founded in 2014.
PHILOSOPHY This producer uses local ingredients and climate to its advantage, highlighting the regional terroir of Texas in its spirits.

The spirit This has been named "Texas straight bourbon whiskey" because it is aged for less than two years, and so is younger than the average bourbon. The grain blend from which it is made contains 70 percent local corn.

The taste Deep amber in color, this spirit oozes notes of vanilla and brown sugar on the nose, and caramel, toffee, and cinnamon on the palate.

Redbreast 12 Year

Irish whiskey, 40% ABV

DISTILLERY Midleton Distillery, County Cork, Ireland. Founded in 1966.
PHILOSOPHY This acclaimed producer creates a unique product that is often regarded as the definitive expression of traditional pot-still Irish whiskey.

The spirit Made from a mash of malted and unmalted barley and then triple-distilled in traditional copper pot stills, this whiskey benefits from an aging process in Oloroso sherry barrels.

The taste A wonderful creamy mouthfeel gives way to spicy, fruity notes with a trademark Christmas-cake-flavored character.

Springbank 10 Year

Scotch whisky, 46% ABV

DISTILLERY Springbank Distillery, Campbeltown, Scotland. Founded in 1828.
PHILOSOPHY Scotland's oldest independent family-owned distillery produces small batches of whisky, using handcrafted methods throughout the process.

The spirit Springbank does 100 percent of the production process on site—rare for Scottish distilleries—and does not buy any additional malt. Lightly peated and distilled two-and-a-half times, this whisky undergoes an exceptionally long fermentation period.

The taste This balanced and full-bodied whisky offers a complex experience for the senses, full of mature flavors and intense aromas.

Stagg Jr.

Bourbon whiskey, 64–67% ABV

DISTILLERY Buffalo Trace Distillery, Kentucky, USA. Spirit launched in 2013.
PHILOSOPHY One of Kentucky's most famous and historic distilleries honors George T. Stagg, who built the most dominant American distillery of the nineteenth century.

The spirit Each batch of this bourbon is unique, hence the varying proofs. Uncut and unfiltered, this big, bold spirit is bottled at barrel proof after aging for nearly a decade in new charred oak barrels.

The taste Rich notes of chocolate and brown sugar mingle in perfect balance with rye spiciness and a smokiness from the barrels.

A trademark pair of antlers signifies the historic Stagg brand

The proof varies, as each batch is unique and no water is added

HOW TO ENJOY
Try neat, but if it burns, add a splash of water.

Stalk & Barrel Single Malt

Whisky, 46% ABV

DISTILLERY Still Waters Distillery, Ontario, Canada. Founded in 2009.
PHILOSOPHY Making whisky in small batches by hand, from grain to glass.

The spirit Made from 100 percent Canadian malted barley, this spirit is mashed, fermented, and then distilled in a small copper pot still. Aging occurs in used bourbon barrels for a minimum of three years.

The taste Varying from batch to batch, this spirit usually features a combination of maltiness and fruit on the nose, with notes of green apple, grape notes, and malt on the palate.

Sullivans Cove Double Cask

Whisky, 40% ABV

DISTILLERY Tasmania Distillery, Tasmania, Australia. Founded in 1994.
PHILOSOPHY Operating on a small scale, this island producer uses only local ingredients to make its spirits, and everything is done by hand.

The spirit Malted Tasmanian barley is brewed in a stainless-steel tank with a combination of brewer's and distiller's yeast, then double-distilled in a copper pot still before being matured in used American oak bourbon and French oak Port barrels.

The taste Well-rounded, with a soft, creamy mouthfeel, this whisky gives off scents of vanilla, fruit, spice, and cloves.

Teeling Small Batch

Irish whiskey, 46% ABV

DISTILLERY Teeling Whiskey Distillery, Dublin, Ireland. Founded in 2013.
PHILOSOPHY Staying true to its family tradition of "quality over quantity", this distillery sports a commitment to forging an innovative new future for Irish whiskey.

The spirit This small-batch bottling consists of hand-selected whiskey barrels, which are initially matured for up to six years in used bourbon barrels, and are then given further maturation in used rum barrels for additional character.

The taste The inviting nose features sweet notes similar to those of rum. On the palate, the smooth liquid gives off notes of wood and spice.

Two James Rye Dog

Rye whiskey, 50.5% ABV

DISTILLERY Two James Spirits, Michigan, USA. Founded in 2013.
PHILOSOPHY This distillery—the first one to be licensed in the city of Detroit since Prohibition—creates spirits using locally sourced ingredients.

The spirit Each batch of this unaged "field-to-bottle" whiskey is made from at least 1,000lb (450kg) of milled, locally grown rye grain. After fermentation, the mash is distilled in a custom-made, 500-gallon (2,200-liter) copper pot still.

The taste This young spirit possesses real character, with floral and citrus notes and a round mouthfeel.

Tycho's Star Single Malt

Whisky, 41.8% ABV

DISTILLERY Spirit of Hven Distillery, Sankt Ibb, Sweden. Founded in 2008.
PHILOSOPHY One of Europe's smallest family-owned distilleries is committed to using organic, sustainable practices.

The spirit This whisky is crafted from three varieties of barley, which are malted, mashed, and fermented. After a double-distillation, the producers age the spirit in three types of oak.

The taste The scent of barley is complemented by notes of coconut and almonds, with tastes of smoke and malt on the palate.

Tyrconnell

Irish whiskey, 40% ABV

DISTILLERY The Kilbeggan Distillery, Leinster, Ireland. Founded in 1757.
PHILOSOPHY Using a unique distillation process to create one of the few Irish single malts.

The spirit Irish malted barley is steeped in water to germinate; after one to two weeks the malt goes to dry in a kiln, and is then milled and added with hot water to a mash tun. After fermentation and distillation, the spirit is gently matured in seasoned oak barrels.

The taste Golden yellow and full of fruity, spicy aromas, this spirit yields flavors of oranges and lemons, with a strong malt presence.

White Oak Akashi

Whisky, 46% ABV

DISTILLERY White Oak Distillery, Hyōgo, Japan. Founded in 1888.
PHILOSOPHY The first distillery in Japan to obtain a whisky license (in 1919) was influenced by Scottish whisky and successfully brought technology and craft to Japan.

The spirit Located near the sea, this distillery enjoys a mild climate—perfect for whisky. Produced in small batches, the spirit is made from a malt sourced from the UK, and water that is typically used in sake production.

The taste This smooth spirit is packed with notes of yellow apple, powdered sugar, and angelica fruit.

WhistlePig 10 Year

Rye whiskey, 50% ABV

DISTILLERY WhistlePig Distillery, Vermont, USA. Spirit launched in 2010.
PHILOSOPHY This distillery—situated on an idyllic farm—believes that rye holds the greatest distilling potential of all grains.

The spirit WhistlePig conducts the entire process in one place, growing and harvesting the rye. After distillation, the spirit undergoes a double-barrel aging process—first in charred new oak barrels and then in barrels made from Vermont oak trees that are logged on the farm.

The taste This whiskey offers aromas of allspice, orange peel, anise, and oak, notes of caramel, vanilla, and mint with a long, sweet finish.

White Pike

Whiskey, 40% ABV

DISTILLERY Finger Lakes Distilling, New York, USA. Founded in 2008.
PHILOSOPHY This innovative producer proudly uses local ingredients and, most notably, ages this spirit for just 18 minutes.

The spirit This clear, white whiskey was created to give cocktails oomph. The team processes and distills local corn, spelt, and malted wheat in custom-made pot and column stills.

The taste This spirit features sweetness from the corn, creaminess from the spelt, and dryness from the malted wheat.

Wigle Organic

Rye whiskey, 46% ABV

DISTILLERY Wigle Whiskey Distillery, Pennsylvania, USA. Founded in 2012.
PHILOSOPHY This community-minded producer strives to create the best organic spirits using creative practices and local ingredients.

The spirit This traditional Monongahela-style rye whiskey is made from local, organic grains that the producer mills on site. Small-batch distillation takes place in a traditional copper pot still, and each batch is barrelled in small, charred oak barrels for over a year.

The taste Spicy rye characteristics run through the experience, with notes of vanilla, maple, brown sugar, and cherry peeking through.

Woodinville Straight

Bourbon whiskey, 45% ABV

DISTILLERY Woodinville Whiskey Co., Washington, USA. Founded in 2010.
PHILOSOPHY Creating spirits by hand from Washington-grown agricultural produce.

The spirit This small-batch bourbon starts with traditionally grown corn, rye, and malted barley, all of which are exclusively cultivated for the distillery on a local family-owned farm. The team mashes the grains, and distills and barrels them on site, then ages the spirit in seasoned oak barrels.

The taste Aromas of crème brûlée and spice delight the nose. The palate responds to notes of rich caramel, dark chocolate, and vanilla pods.

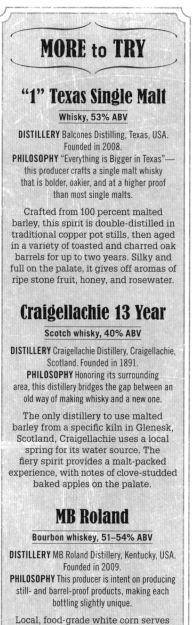

MORE to TRY

"1" Texas Single Malt

Whisky, 53% ABV

DISTILLERY Balcones Distilling, Texas, USA. Founded in 2008.
PHILOSOPHY "Everything is Bigger in Texas"— this producer crafts a single malt whisky that is bolder, oakier, and at a higher proof than most single malts.

Crafted from 100 percent malted barley, this spirit is double-distilled in traditional copper pot stills, then aged in a variety of toasted and charred oak barrels for up to two years. Silky and full on the palate, it gives off aromas of ripe stone fruit, honey, and rosewater.

Craigellachie 13 Year

Scotch whisky, 40% ABV

DISTILLERY Craigellachie Distillery, Craigellachie, Scotland. Founded in 1891.
PHILOSOPHY Honoring its surrounding area, this distillery bridges the gap between an old way of making whisky and a new one.

The only distillery to use malted barley from a specific kiln in Glenesk, Scotland, Craigellachie uses a local spring for its water source. The fiery spirit provides a malt-packed experience, with notes of clove-studded baked apples on the palate.

MB Roland

Bourbon whiskey, 51–54% ABV

DISTILLERY MB Roland Distillery, Kentucky, USA. Founded in 2009.
PHILOSOPHY This producer is intent on producing still- and barrel-proof products, making each bottling slightly unique.

Local, food-grade white corn serves as the bedrock of this product, which is bottled at distillation and barrel-proofed in the style of a pre-Prohibition bourbon. This unique, full-flavored expression has sweet caramel and honey notes on the nose and palate, with a hint of cinnamon in the finish.

Infusing Whisky, Bourbon, and Rye

Your goal when infusing whisky isn't to mask its flavor, but rather to complement it. Avoid using an aged, expressive whisky or Scotch, which will dominate almost any infusion— mellow bourbons and rye whiskies are the best choices. Choose from a range of ingredients, and follow the best method on pages 24–25.

Bacon

Wow your friends with a smoky bacon infusion—whisky and bourbon pair beautifully with bacon.

What you need 3–4 slices smoked or cured bacon; 3 cups whisky.

Infusing time 2 days; store for one day at room temperature, then strain the whisky and store for another day in the fridge or freezer.

The next level Add 1–2 tbsp maple syrup to add a sweet note to the infusion.

Fig

To take your Manhattan cocktail to the next level, pair a mellow bourbon with rich, sweet figs.

What you need 12 small, fresh figs; 3 cups whisky.

Infusing time 2–3 weeks.

The next level Try adding ½ vanilla pod for another flavor component.

Coffee

Add a caffeinated kick by infusing a smooth whisky or bourbon with coffee.

What you need 4oz (115g) espresso-roast coffee beans, crushed; 3 cups whisky.

Infusing time 2–3 weeks.

The next level Add ½ vanilla pod to soften any acidic characteristics.

Cinnamon–Chile

Spicy cinnamon-flavored whisky has taken the world by storm—it is easy to make your own.

What you need 8 cinnamon sticks; 3–6 whole dried red chile peppers (depending on your tolerance); 3 cups whisky.

Infusing time 1–2 days.

The next level To take some of the sting out and gain a more rounded flavor, add 1 tbsp simple syrup or agave syrup.

Sweet Potato

Give your whisky an earthy yet sweet note by infusing with sweet potatoes.

What you need 1 large, mature sweet potato, peeled and cut into chunks; 3 cups whisky.

Infusing time 1–2 weeks.

The next level Add a cinnamon stick to the jar for an autumnal finished product. If the whisky masks the sweetness of the sweet potato, add 1 tbsp agave syrup or simple syrup.

Blackberry

Sweeten up your whisky or bourbon by infusing with fresh blackberries.

What you need 8oz (225g) blackberries; 3 cups whisky.

Infusing time 3–5 days.

The next level Add the peel of one lemon (pith removed) for a tart citrus note. If you are using the bourbon to make Mint Juleps, add a handful of fresh mint sprigs into the infusion with the berries.

Mint Julep

The Mint Julep is a sweet cocktail that plays on the delicious pairing of mint and whisky. The name Julep derives from the Persian word *Golâb*, meaning rosewater, and it is traditionally known as a medicinal drink. You can make Juleps with most spirits, but the Mint Julep is perfect for bourbon whiskey – and a great introduction to creating whisky cocktails.

The Classic Recipe

Good-quality ingredients are key. Some purists avoid agitating the mint, but gentle muddling is the best way to release the herb's oils.

1 Place 6 mint leaves in a double old-fashioned glass.

2 Add 1 tablespoon simple syrup.

3 Pack the glass with crushed ice.

4 Pour in 2fl oz (60ml) bourbon. Use a bar spoon to stir well until the glass is frosted.

Serve it up Repack the glass with ice and garnish with fresh mint sprigs.

Create Your Own Signature Mix

Key Components

1 Place **6 mint leaves** in the glass.

Traditionally, the drink calls for spearmint, but most varieties of mint work. Serve extra mint alongside the drink for those who want to add the herb to their cocktail.

2 Add **1 tablespoon simple syrup**.

Flavor your simple syrup with mint extract (see p27). You could also pour your bourbon over a sugar cube and then muddle it with fresh mint.

3 Pack the glass with **crushed ice**.

You must serve this extra-cold. Use crushed ice to ensure you can pack the drink—pebbled ice is also a good choice.

4 Pour in **2fl oz (60ml) bourbon**. Use a bar spoon to stir well.

Choose a Kentucky bourbon, preferably overproof. If you haven't acquired a taste for the spirit, seek a young wheat variety; if you're looking for more character, try a spicy rye.

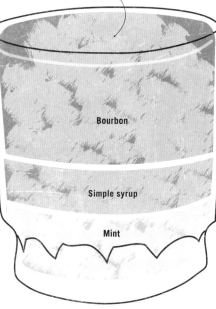

Crushed ice

Bourbon

Simple syrup

Mint

Additional Flourishes

Garnish Rest fresh mint on the ice for proximity to the nose; the scent adds to the overall experience. You could also add other herbs, such as basil, in the same way.

Fruit For fruit flavor, muddle 1 tablespoon of macerated fruit, such as strawberries, with the mint and simple syrup.

Craft Reinventions

The Julep rewards experimentation. Some mixologists substitute their favorite whisky and fresh herbs, or add more sweetness with fresh fruit to minimize the bourbon hit. Here are three Mint Juleps, reimagined.

Peach Julep Fizz

In a shaker, muddle the mint, juice, and syrup. Add the bourbon and stir. Pour into a collins glass, pack with ice, and top up with soda. Stir, top up the ice, and add the peach and mint. Serve.

- mint sprig and peach slice
- 3fl oz (90ml) soda
- 2fl oz (60ml) bourbon
- 1 tbsp simple syrup
- 1 tbsp peach juice
- 8 mint leaves

Basil Ginger Whiskey Julep

In a shaker, muddle the basil and syrup. Add the whiskey and stir. Strain into a double old-fashioned glass, and pack with ice. Stir, and top up the ice. Top with the ginger and basil, and serve.

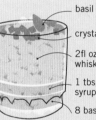

- basil leaf
- crystallized ginger
- 2fl oz (60ml) Irish whiskey
- 1 tbsp ginger simple syrup
- 8 basil leaves

◀ Blackberry Mint Julep

In a shaker, muddle the mint, berries, and syrup. Add the bourbon and stir. Pour into a double old-fashioned glass and pack with ice. Stir, top up the ice, and add the mint and blackberry. Serve.

- mint sprig and blackberry
- 2fl oz (60ml) bourbon
- 1 tbsp mint simple syrup
- 6 blackberries
- 8 mint leaves

Sazerac

The Sazerac is the most famous drink to have emerged from New Orleans' renowned cocktail history. The original was made with Cognac, but bartenders today use rye whiskey and a dash of absinthe. It is considered to be the oldest known American cocktail, dating back to pre-Civil War New Orleans—making it ripe for a contemporary update.

The Classic Recipe

The most unique characteristic of this drink is the absinthe wash.

1 Fill a double old-fashioned glass with ice. Muddle a sugar cube and 2 dashes Peychaud's bitters in a mixing glass.

2 Add 2fl oz (60ml) rye whiskey and ice to the mixing glass, and stir until chilled.

3 Discard the ice from the first glass. Pour in 1½ tsp absinthe, swirl to coat the inside of the glass, and then discard the absinthe. Strain the mixture into the first glass.

Serve it up Twist a lemon peel over the top, then discard it.

Create Your Own Signature Mix

Key Components

1 Muddle a **sugar cube** and **2 dashes Peychaud's bitters** in a mixing glass.

Peychaud's bitters are lighter and sweeter than Angostura bitters. You could also try spicy or fruit-flavored bitters.

2 Add **2fl oz (60ml) rye whiskey** and ice, and stir.

If you don't like the spiciness of rye, consider swapping it for a smooth Cognac. Bourbon and wheat whiskey are also fun alternatives.

3 Pour **1½ tsp absinthe** into your double old-fashioned glass. Swirl to coat, and then discard. Strain the mixture into the rinsed glass.

It may seem ceremonial, but the absinthe wash is a crucial feature. For a change, try rinsing with Herbsaint or Pernod.

Additional Flourishes

Garnish Some believe you should discard the lemon twist after you squeeze it over the drink; others decorate with a lemon wedge or curl.

Citrus If you find the classic is a bit strong, add 1 teaspoon fresh lemon juice—the acidity cuts through the alcohol's punch.

Rye whiskey

Bitters

Sugar cube

Absinthe

Craft Reinventions

The classic version has a unique smoky citrus flavor profile—mixologists depart from tradition by adding in contrasting flavor notes with spicy or sweet ingredients. Take your pick from the three unique variations on the right.

Spicy Sazerac

Rinse a double old-fashioned glass with absinthe (see the classic). In a glass, mix the bourbon, bitters, syrup, and ice. Stir until cold, and strain into the first glass. Twist over a lemon peel, discard. Serve.

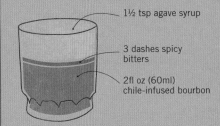

1½ tsp agave syrup

3 dashes spicy bitters

2fl oz (60ml) chile-infused bourbon

Smoky Sazerac

Rinse a double old-fashioned glass with absinthe (see the classic). Add a smoky ice cube (see p29). In a glass, stir the liquid ingredients with ice, and strain into the first glass. Add the peel. Serve.

lemon peel

1 tbsp simple syrup

1½ tsp fresh lemon juice

2 dashes Peychaud's bitters

2fl oz (60ml) rye whiskey

◀ Maple Sazerac

Rinse a double old-fashioned glass with sweet vermouth (see the classic, as with absinthe). In a glass, stir the rye, bitters, juice, syrup, and ice, and pour it into the first glass. Add the twist. Serve.

lemon twist

1 tbsp maple syrup

1½ tsp fresh lemon juice

2 dashes Angostura bitters

2fl oz (60ml) rye whiskey

Manhattan

The Manhattan was one of the first cocktails to combine rye with vermouth. Once considered the most masculine of drinks, the boozy New York cocktail appeals to a wider audience today. It has enjoyed a revival thanks to a renewed focus on full-flavored, hand-crafted spirits and exciting ideas from today's craft spirit enthusiasts.

The Classic Recipe

The Manhattan has a flavor profile that is two-thirds booze and one-third sweet. For best results, serve it cold.

1 Pour 2fl oz (60ml) rye whiskey into a mixing glass.

2 Add ¾fl oz (20ml) sweet vermouth.

3 Top with 2 dashes Angostura bitters.

4 Add ice cubes, and stir until chilled. Strain the mixture into a chilled Martini glass.

Serve it up Top with a maraschino cherry.

Create Your Own Signature Mix

Key Components

1 Pour **2fl oz (60ml) rye whiskey** into a mixing glass.

Rye usually forms the base, but you could try a craft Canadian whiskey or bourbon whiskey instead.

2 Add **¾fl oz (20ml) sweet vermouth**.

Sweet vermouth offers a sweet counterpart to the alcohol. You can also splash in a little of the maraschino cherry juice to mellow the alcoholic notes.

3 Top with **2 dashes Angostura bitters**.

You can completely transform a classic Manhattan by using an offbeat flavor of bitters. Try Peychaud's or a sweeter bitters instead of Angostura.

4 Add **ice cubes**, and stir until chilled. Strain into your glass.

As with most booze-forward drinks, it is very important to stir with ice so that it is extra cold. You could pour the drink over a large, flavor-infused cube. This imparts a flavor as the ice melts.

Bitters

Rye whiskey

Sweet vermouth

Additional Flourishes

Garnish A maraschino cherry is the classic garnish, but you could drop a fresh cherry into the base of the glass for a tart sweetness, or a sour cherry for an extra kick.

Froth Try shaking the ingredients with ice instead of stirring; this will lead to an aerated, frothy texture.

Craft Reinventions

Bartenders make Manhattans with nearly any spirit. Some work much better than others. If you have a favorite spirit, try giving it the Manhattan treatment and see what you think. On the right are three tried-and-tested versions.

Tequila Manhattan

In a mixing glass, combine the tequila, vermouth, and bitters. Add ice cubes, and stir until chilled. Strain into a chilled Martini glass. Garnish with a cherry, and serve.

- maraschino cherry
- 2 dashes Angostura bitters
- ³/₄fl oz (20ml) sweet vermouth
- 2fl oz (60ml) aged tequila

Cuban Manhattan

In a mixing glass, combine the rum, vermouth, and bitters. Add ice cubes, and stir until chilled. Strain into a chilled Martini glass. Garnish with an orange twist, and serve.

- orange twist
- 3 dashes Peychaud's bitters
- ³/₄fl oz (20ml) sweet vermouth
- 2fl oz (60ml) aged rum

◄ Brandy Manhattan

In a mixing glass, combine the brandy, vermouth, juice, and bitters. Add ice cubes, and stir until chilled. Place a cherry into a Martini glass. Strain over the mixture. Top with lemon, and serve.

- maraschino cherry and lemon twist
- 2 dashes Angostura bitters
- 1¹/₂ tsp maraschino cherry juice
- 1 tbsp sweet vermouth
- 2fl oz (60ml) brandy

Old Fashioned

The Old Fashioned is one of the original American cocktails, dating back to the nineteenth century. Generations of cocktail lovers have made it their favorite. Some recipes call for whisky, brandy, or gin as the base, and these days the drink usually features bourbon. It is rewarding to create new versions while remaining true to the drink's roots.

The Classic Recipe

You need nothing more than bourbon (or rye) whiskey, bitters, sugar, and a citrus peel for this simple favorite.

1 Place a sugar cube in a double old-fashioned glass. Pour 2 dashes Angostura bitters onto the cube, then a dash of water.

2 Add 2fl oz (60ml) bourbon.

3 Add a handful of ice cubes. Stir rapidly until chilled.

Serve it up Garnish with an orange twist and a cherry.

Create Your Own Signature Mix

Key Components

1 Place a **sugar cube** in your glass. Pour **2 dashes Angostura bitters** onto the cube, then a **dash of water**.

A bitters-soaked sugar cube is the old-school sweet base. You could use superfine sugar—it dissolves better. For a sweeter drink, muddle the cherry and/or orange twist into the sugar and bitters.

2 Add **2fl oz (60ml) bourbon.**

Bourbon is the most common base, although you could opt for a craft rye whiskey or Canadian whiskey.

3 Add a handful of **ice cubes**. Stir rapidly until chilled.

Such a booze-forward cocktail should be cold. You can add citrus or liquid smoke to your ice cube tray (see p29); the flavors will change character as the cubes melt.

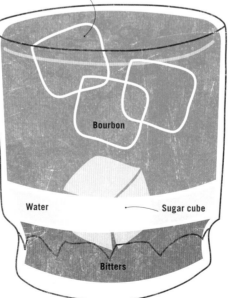

Ice cubes

Bourbon

Water

Sugar cube

Bitters

Additional Flourishes

Lemon peel Try muddling fresh lemon or lime peel with the sugar cube before adding the bitters. It reduces the potency of the alcohol flavors.

Bitters Seek an alternative to classic Angostura. Try exotic flavors, such as black walnut or West Indian orange.

Bubbles For a fizzy alternative, add a splash of soda on your sugar cube instead of water.

Craft Reinventions

Update the classic with these variations. Some bartenders make Old Fashioneds with rum, brandy, or gin, returning to recipes of old. Stick with bourbon and you can reimagine the drink using a range of bitters, garnishes, and liqueurs.

Fizzy Fruity Old Fashioned

Place a sugar cube in a glass. Pour in the bitters, then add fruit and muddle. Add bourbon and soda, and strain into an ice-filled double old-fashioned glass. Stir. Top with the twist and cherry. Serve.

orange twist
maraschino cherry
1fl oz (30ml) soda

2fl oz (60ml) bourbon

2 dashes Angostura bitters with an orange slice and cherry

Rum Old Fashioned

Combine the bitters, syrup, and rum in a glass. Add ice cubes, and stir rapidly until chilled. Strain into an ice-filled double old-fashioned glass. Garnish with a twist, and serve.

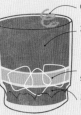

orange twist

2fl oz (60ml) aged rum

1 tbsp brown sugar simple syrup

2 dashes Peychaud's bitters

◄ Coffee Old Fashioned

Combine the bitters, syrup, crème de cacao, and bourbon in a shaker. Add ice and shake for 10 seconds. Strain into an ice-filled double old-fashioned glass, top with coffee and chocolate, and serve.

grated white chocolate

1½fl oz (45ml) cold-brewed coffee
2fl oz (60ml) bourbon
1 tbsp crème de cacao
1 tbsp simple syrup
2 dashes orange bitters

Blood and Sand

The Blood and Sand is probably the best-known Scotch cocktail. It was created for the 1922 silent movie starring Rudolph Valentino—the cocktail's color was thought by some to resemble blood. Fruity and not too smoky, it's a great gateway experience for people who normally don't enjoy Scotch, and perfect for updating with modern flavors.

The Classic Recipe

It may sound complex, but this is easy to make: simply shake and stir equal measures of each ingredient.

1 Pour 1fl oz (30ml) Scotch whisky into a shaker.

2 Pour in 1fl oz (30ml) sweet vermouth.

3 Add 1fl oz (30ml) cherry brandy.

4 Add 1fl oz (30ml) fresh orange juice.

5 Fill to the top with ice, and shake for 10 seconds. Strain the mixture into a chilled Martini glass.

Serve it up Garnish with orange peel and a maraschino cherry.

Create Your Own Signature Mix

Key Components

1 Pour **1fl oz (30ml) Scotch whisky** into a shaker.

Stick to a gentle, blended Scotch—it will shine through. Avoid using a strong, peaty Scotch unless you're a big fan of such flavors.

2 Pour in **1fl oz (30ml) sweet vermouth**.

This combines with the liqueur and orange juice to combat the Scotch. You can tweak to find the balance of sweet–smoky you like—if you prefer, swap out sweet vermouth with dry.

3 Add **1fl oz (30ml) cherry brandy**.

Use a cherry liqueur for a sweeter take.

4 Add **1fl oz (30ml) fresh orange juice**.

Blood orange juice gives extra flavor and color.

5 Fill to the top with **ice cubes**, and shake for 10 seconds. Strain the mixture into your glass.

Serving it extra-cold provides a very smooth experience. If the finished product is too strong, you may wish to add a large ice cube to the glass.

Orange juice

Cherry brandy

Scotch whisky

Sweet vermouth

Additional Flourishes

Garnish Consider using booze-soaked maraschino cherries. Simply soak the cherries in a small amount of Scotch overnight and pop one in your cocktail. Help to keep the drink cool by freezing the soaked berries and adding one to the drink.

Flamed peel Enhance the burnt orange flavors of the drink by garnishing with a strip of flamed peel instead of a fresh one (see p29).

Craft Reinventions

The classic version is limited to four ingredients, but many bartenders expand the recipe, adding bitters and unusual liqueurs. The variations on the right produce incredible results and remain true to the original.

New Blood, Old Sand

In a mixing glass, combine the sherry, vermouth, liqueurs, bitters, and juice. Fill with ice, and stir until the mixture is cold. Strain into a chilled coupe glass, garnish with the cherry, and serve.

- rum-soaked cherry
- ¾fl oz (20ml) fresh blood orange juice
- 1 dash Angostura bitters
- 1½ tsp each Cynar and Luxardo liqueurs
- ¾fl oz (20ml) sweet vermouth
- 2fl oz (60ml) fino sherry

Bitter Blood and Sand

In a shaker, mix the Scotch, vermouth, liqueur, juices, and bitters. Fill with ice and shake for 10 seconds. Strain into a chilled Martini glass, garnish with the orange and cherry, and serve.

- slice of orange and a maraschino cherry
- 2 dashes Angostura bitters
- ¾fl oz (20ml) each of orange and lemon juice
- ¾fl oz (20ml) cherry liqueur
- 1fl oz (30ml) bitter vermouth
- 1fl oz (30ml) Scotch

◄ Extra Bloody Blood and Sand

In a shaker, mix the Scotch, vermouth, liqueur, and juices. Fill with ice, and shake for 10 seconds. Strain into a chilled Martini glass, top with the orange wheel and cherry, and serve.

- flamed orange wheel and a maraschino cherry
- 1fl oz (30ml) blood orange juice
- 1½ tsp maraschino cherry juice
- 1fl oz (30ml) cherry liqueur
- 1fl oz (30ml) sweet vermouth
- 1fl oz (30ml) Scotch

Rum is distilled from **sugar-cane** by-products, such as molasses. Producers also distill directly from sugar-cane juice, and this variety—traditionally a product of the French Caribbean—is known as rhum agricole. **Naturally sweet** and clear, most high-quality rum is aged. The longer it ages for, the darker in color and more **expressive** it can become, thanks to prolonged contact with **wooden barrels**. It was once almost exclusively produced on **tropical** islands, but today producers all over the world can access good-quality sugar cane to make the spirit. Rum remains a **key ingredient** in most tropical tiki cocktails, but many consumers today also **appreciate craft rums**—such as those on the following pages—in the way they would a sipping whisky. Explore for yourself, then try **pushing boundaries** by creating your own sweet–sour cocktails or complementary infusions.

RUM

Balcones Texas

Rum, 63.9% ABV

DISTILLERY Balcones Distilling, Texas, USA. Spirit launched in 2013.
PHILOSOPHY As the famous saying goes: "Everything is Bigger in Texas." This producer aims big, using whisky-making techniques to create rum.

The spirit The producer ferments two types of premium molasses, then distills them twice in hand-built copper pot stills. After aging in a variety of oak barrels, the rum is bottled at cask strength.

The taste As rich and expressive as a whisky, this rum contains elements of maple syrup, leather, burnt marshmallow, cacao, hazelnut, and tart cherry skins.

Batavia-Arrack van Oosten

Arrack, 50% ABV

DISTILLERY Dutch East Indies Trading, Jakarta, Indonesia. Spirit launched in 1901.
PHILOSOPHY This Indonesian producer distills traditional Arrack—a historic cane spirit that is a key ingredient in many classic punch recipes.

The spirit The team uses fermented red rice to start the sugar-cane fermentation. The resulting wash is then distilled and stored in vats made of local hardwood that impart a distinctive flavor.

The taste The nose is similar to that of a classic rum, but there are distinct notes of wood, smoke, and flowers.

Bayou Select

Rum, 40% ABV

DISTILLERY Louisiana Spirits Distillery, Louisiana, USA. Founded in 2011.
PHILOSOPHY This small producer uses local ingredients to celebrate the vibrant agricultural culture of the area.

The spirit Louisiana produces more sugar cane than any Caribbean island. The team produces rum from local molasses and raw sugar, then ages it for up to three years in American oak bourbon barrels in the Louisiana heat.

The taste Sweet and rich, this rum offers notes of cherry, cocoa, and oak.

HOW TO ENJOY The strong flavors work in chocolate- or coffee-based cocktails.

Bully Boy White

Rum, 40% ABV

DISTILLERY Bully Boy Distillers, Massachusetts, USA. Founded in 2011.
PHILOSOPHY These upstart producers transform white rum—historically, a relatively neutral spirit—by crafting a bold-flavored variety.

The spirit Blackstrap molasses is mixed with water and fermented for 7–10 days, giving the rum full notes of flavor. The spirit is pulled from the still at 180 proof, and is then cut to proof with filtered water.

The taste This rum has a light-to-medium body with distinctive burnt sugar, vanilla, and pineapple notes, and a smooth finish.

Beenleigh White

Rum, 37.5% ABV

DISTILLERY Beenleigh Artisan Distillery, Queensland, Australia. Founded in 1884.
PHILOSOPHY Making rum using traditional methods, this is the first registered distillery in Australia and the longest continuously in service.

The spirit A mix of pure Queensland rainwater, locally sourced molasses, and proprietary yeast is processed in the distillery's original copper pot still. The rum matures for two years in small used brandy vats, then passes through carbon filters.

The taste Along with a soft mouthfeel and a smooth finish, this distinctive, luscious rum offers hints of vanilla, oak, and molasses.

Bundaberg

Rum, 37% ABV

DISTILLERY The Bundaberg Distilling Company, Queensland, Australia. Founded in 1888.
PHILOSOPHY A time-honored production process and the local rich, volcanic soil lend a unique flavor to this rum.

The spirit Fresh molasses is piped directly from the mill to the distillery, where it is placed in storage wells. It is diluted with water, clarified, and diluted again, before fermenting for 36 hours. The staff distills the resulting wash in a column still, and then a pot still. The rum ages in white oak vats for at least two years.

The taste This rum is light and sweet on the nose. There are flavors of freshly rolled tobacco and burnt sugar cane.

Caña Brava

Rum, 43% ABV

DISTILLERY Las Cabras Distillery, Herrera, Panamá. Spirit launched in 2012.
PHILOSOPHY Using traditional methods to produce a dry blanca rum that has similarities with legendary pre-Revolution Cuban rums.

The spirit The staff process locally grown sugar cane into sugar and molasses within 24 hours of harvest to preserve freshness. Fermented with pineapple yeast, the spirit is distilled in a copper and brass continuous still, then aged in bourbon barrels for two to three years. Carbon-filtered, the spirit is aged in used whisky barrels for three years, then filtered again, and cut to proof.

The taste Clean and fresh, this rum offers notes of sugar cane, citrus, and oak. The smooth spirit carries elements of vanilla and dark chocolate.

Clément VSOP

Rum, 40% ABV

DISTILLERY Habitation Clément, Le Francois, Martinique. Founded in 1887.
PHILOSOPHY To further the company's longstanding position as a pioneer of aged rhum agricole by balancing tradition and modernity.

The spirit The producer harvests state-grown spring sugar cane and crushes it on the same day for maximum freshness. After the pressed sugar-cane juice has fermented into a sugar-cane wine, it is distilled in a Créole copper column still, vat-conditioned, and aged in oak barrels.

The taste This complex, deep amber rhum offers aromas of roasted almonds, suede, and salted butter. The dry, full body tastes of dried fruit, spice, pepper, and tobacco.

Crusoe Organic Spiced (Greenbar)

Rum, 35% ABV

DISTILLERY Greenbar Craft Distillery, California, USA. Spirit launched in 2009.
PHILOSOPHY This producer's search for clean, bold flavors means it uses exclusively organic ingredients for fermentation.

The spirit Molasses ferments in temperature-controlled tanks using white wine yeast, is distilled, then micro-oxygenated in stainless-steel tanks—this step mellows the rum without the need for barrel-aging or charcoal-filtering, which can strip out flavor.

The taste You can trace flavors from the rum's month-long infusion, such as cinnamon, clove, vanilla, fresh orange zest, and osthmanthus flowers.

Damoiseau VSOP

Rum, 42% ABV

DISTILLERY Distillerie Bellevue, Le Moule, Guadeloupe. Founded in 1942.
PHILOSOPHY For three generations, the Damoiseau family has been producing rhum agricole that is the pride of the island of Guadeloupe.

The spirit After being harvested and crushed on the same day, local sugar-cane juice is fermented for 24–36 hours, then distilled once in a Créole continuous column still. More than four years of aging occurs in charred bourbon barrels.

The taste This amber-colored rhum yields exotic aromas of dried fruits and spices, with a long, peppery finish.

The logo—two running men carrying a barrel between them—was inspired by an infamous break-in at the distillery in 1942

To achieve this deep color, the rhum agricole ages for four years in oak, like many Cognacs and Armagnacs

Depaz Blue Cane

Rum, 45% ABV

DISTILLERY Château Depaz Estate, St. Pierre, Martinique. Founded in 1651.
PHILOSOPHY This historic producer—established by Martinique's first governor—uses coveted and costly blue sugar cane.

The spirit To make rhum agricole, the producer uses seasonal natural sugar-cane juice from each year's crop of blue cane (rather than a standard by-products available all year, such as molasses). Depaz's appellation status ensures its strict adherence to precise standards of production.

The taste This light rhum carries an inviting bouquet of nutmeg and oak. On the palate, sweet, floral flavors contrast with spice, smoke, and vanilla.

Diplomatico Reserva Exclusiva

Rum, 40% ABV

DISTILLERY Destilerías Unidas S. A., Lara State, Venezuela. Founded in 1959.
PHILOSOPHY Using environmentally conscious methods, this producer carefully crafts rum from premium sugar cane.

The spirit Made from fresh local sugar cane, this rum is distilled in ancient copper pot stills and then aged in small oak casks for up to 12 years.

The taste Amber in color, this rum boasts notes of maple syrup, orange peel, brown sugar, and sweet toffee.

HOW TO ENJOY This is an elegant and complex sipping rum.

Don Pancho Origenes 30 Year

Rum, 40% ABV

DISTILLERY Las Cabras Distillery, Herrera, Panamá. Spirit launched 2012.
PHILOSOPHY This rum was developed by Master Blender Francisco "Don Pancho" Fernandez, who has been making rums for more than 50 years.

The spirit Made from molasses and the Master Blender's proprietary yeast, the spirit is distilled in copper column stills (from 1912 and 1922), then aged in both young and mature kinds of American oak bourbon barrels.

The taste With deep aromas of vanilla and oak, this full-bodied rum tastes of figs and bourbon, with a warm finish.

El Dorado 15 Year

Rum, 40% ABV

DISTILLERY Diamond Distillery, East Bank Demerara, Guyana. Spirit launched in 1993.
PHILOSOPHY This producer uses a variety of stills to produce a range of rums that honor Guyana's long history of rum production.

The spirit This aged dark rum is a blend of distillates from four different stills, each made of durable Amazonian Greenheart wood. The blend endows the finished product with a rich and complex character.

The taste This amber-mahogany spirit somewhat resembles a Scotch thanks to its dry, peaty finish and sweet yet smoky notes of tobacco and leather.

English Harbour 5 Year

Rum, 40% ABV

DISTILLERY Antigua Distillery, St. John's, Antigua. Spirit launched in 2001.
PHILOSOPHY This distillery—founded in 1932 by a group of Portuguese rum shop owners—honors the island's rich rum history, which dates back to the early eighteenth century.

The spirit Molasses is fermented for 24–36 hours in open-top fermenters with a combination of wild and commercial yeast. Distillation occurs in a five-column copper continuous still, and the rum is aged in old bourbon barrels.

The taste Round and dry with fruit characteristics, this rum features aromas of molasses, orange rind, and coconut.

Due North

Rum, 40% ABV

DISTILLERY Van Brunt Stillhouse, New York, USA. Founded in 2012.
PHILOSOPHY This Brooklyn producer prides itself in making bold spirits from scratch with a nod to classic styles and innovation.

The spirit Fairtrade, organic sugar cane is harvested from small family farms in the foothills of the Himalayas, and—in its dry and unprocessed form—it is sent to New York. The distillery dissolves it in water before fermentation. The wash is distilled and then aged in new and used charred whisky barrels.

The taste This rich, expressive rum receives notes of vanilla and molasses from the aging process.

Freshwater Michigan

Rum, 40% ABV

DISTILLERY New Holland Artisan Spirits, Michigan, USA. Founded in 2005.
PHILOSOPHY After achieving success in the world of craft beer, this acclaimed producer creates unique and interesting spirits in their most accomplished form.

The spirit Molasses and sugar cane are fermented in-house, then distilled twice in a Prohibition-era still. After the spirit is blended, it is barrel-aged for a minimum of one year.

The taste This rum boasts an aroma of butterscotch and almond. The soft liquid gives off hints of toffee and vanilla, followed by a gentle, spicy finish.

Clément VSOP

Clément VSOP is a rhum agricole, which means "agricultural rum"—a distinctive rum that is crafted on a seasonal basis from freshly pressed sugar-cane juice. It is produced by Rhum Clément at Habitation Clément—a historic independent distillery in Martinique, founded in 1887 by the rhum agricole pioneer, Dr. Homère Clément.

What's the story?

In 1887, the French Caribbean sugar-cane industry was in tatters due to the introduction of sugar beet in Europe. Dr. Homère Clément decided to transform one of the island's most prestigious sugar plantations into a producer of world-class rhum agricole instead of harvesting sugar cane to refine sugar. Traditionally, rum was distilled from molasses, a by-product of sugar cane. Clément's idea was to distill the first-pressed aromatic and full-flavored juice that could be extracted from estate-grown sugar cane to make rhum agricole.

Today, each step of the process, from the harvest of sugar cane and distillation to the aging and bottling process, is conducted by Rhum Clément. Sugar cane is harvested in the spring and crushed the same day for maximum freshness. After the pressed sugar-cane juice has fermented into a "wine," it is distilled once in a copper column still, and rested in vats before being bottled or placed in an oak cask for aging.

What's next?

In light of an increased demand for aged rhum agricole, the distillery is building new cellars to house more barrels. They are also enhancing the range of rhums in the portfolio, experimenting with methods for conditioning oak barrels, and cask finishes.

Founded in
1887
Exported from Martinique in
1923

10 rhums in the line

Above Bagasse (spent sugar cane after it has been crushed) being recirculated for further sugar extraction.

Above A selection of barrels aging in the Clément cellars.

Left Habitation Clément uses column stills for the distillation of rhum agricole.

Who is behind it?

Habitation Clément remained in the Clément family for 100 years. In 1987, it was bought by the Hayot family, who maintain the heritage, culture, and passion of the original distillery. **Robert Peronet** (pictured) has been Cellar Master at Rhum Clément since 1993. He oversees the flavor profile, achieving targeted flavors from various kinds of barrels through conditioning and transfers from one oak barrel to another.

Iridium Gold

Rum, 40% ABV

DISTILLERY Mt. Uncle Distillery, Queensland, Australia. Founded in 2001.
PHILOSOPHY In a remote corner of Australia, this producer uses the best local ingredients and the latest distillation technology to create rum.

The spirit The team ferments a sugar-cane syrup base, then distills it in a copper pot still. For four years, the rum is aged in large, reconditioned American oak hogshead barrels (large barrels traditionally used for tobacco).

The taste This rum has a coveted golden hue and a silky mouthfeel that encourages sip after sip of the sweet vanilla and caramel flavors.

Kō Hana Kea

Rum, 40% ABV

DISTILLERY Manulele Distillers, Kunia, Hawaii. Founded in 2011.
PHILOSOPHY Meticulously crafting spirits from farm to bottle, this producer pays special attention to the unique characteristics of each Kō (sugar cane) varietal.

The spirit This distillery harvests and presses its own sugar cane, and ferments it for over a week with a strain of cacao yeast. After distillation in a combination pot–column still, the agricole-style spirit rests for three months in stainless steel vats.

The taste This crystal-clear rum carries the essence of freshly pressed native Hawaiian sugar cane, with elements of banana, fresh cream, and butterscotch.

Maelstrom

Rum, 42% ABV

DISTILLERY 11 Wells Spirits, Minnesota, USA. Founded in 2012.
PHILOSOPHY To express the characteristics of each ingredient as simply and purely as possible.

The spirit This is an agricole-style rum, which preserves the fresh-picked flavor of unadulterated sugar-cane juice. The producer ferments the juice with Champagne yeast at an ambient temperature. Distillation occurs in a 250-gallon (1,100-liter) octagonal-sided still, then continues in a four-plate column still.

The taste On the nose and palate, this rum exudes light, sweet, and floral notes of sugar cane, with lingering flavors of citrus.

Owney's NYC

Rum, 40% ABV

DISTILLERY The Noble Experiment, New York, USA. Founded in 2012.
PHILOSOPHY To showcase the power of the finest ingredients and a meticulous attention to detail during production.

The spirit This producer carries out the whole production process on-site at a small distillery—mashing, fermenting, distilling, bottling, and labeling. Natural, non-GMO sugar-cane molasses ferments for five days in cold tanks, before it is distilled in a pot–column hybrid still.

The taste Floral on the nose, this silky rum balances tropical fruit flavors with smoky notes and a dry finish.

Montanya Platino

Rum, 40% ABV

DISTILLERY Montanya Distillers, Colorado, USA. Founded in 2008.
PHILOSOPHY Situated in the heart of the Rocky Mountains, this craft rum distillery uses old-world artisan traditions, combining science with art.

The spirit Pure sugar cane and mountain spring water forms the base. After at least a week of fermentation, the wash goes into copper pot stills. The distiller ages the spirit in American oak barrels, filters it through coconut-husk charcoal, and blends it with Colorado mountain spring water.

The taste This rum's body and gentle vanilla scent are complemented by notes of honey, vanilla, and dried fruit.

Penny Blue XO Single Estate

Rum, 44% ABV

DISTILLERY Medine Distillery, Black River, Mauritius. Spirit launched in 2013.
PHILOSOPHY Each limited-edition batch of this single-estate, hand-crafted rum is selected by hand by two Master Blenders.

The spirit Made with sugar cane grown on site, this rum is distilled in a column still, then aged in a combination of Cognac, bourbon, and whisky barrels. Blended from 14 individual casks, each batch is aged for around seven years.

The taste Rich, smooth, and fruity, this rum smells of citrus and orange blossom and tastes of espresso, clove, and honey.

Pink Pigeon

Rum, 40% ABV

DISTILLERY Medine Distillery, Black River, Mauritius. Spirit launched in 2011.
PHILOSOPHY Unique ingredients are used to produce a single-estate, handcrafted rum named after a local bird—one of the world's rarest.

The spirit This spiced rum is deliberately unaged to encourage a smooth and light canvas for a unique blend of three locally sourced flavor infusions: natural bourbon vanilla, orange citrus, and orchid petals from Réunion Island.

The taste The rum has a rich and creamy texture, and features unusual flavor notes of tropical fruits and sweet spices.

Pusser's Blue Label

Rum, 40% ABV

DISTILLERY Diamond Distillery, Georgetown, Guyana; Angostura Distillery, Port of Spain, Trinidad. Spirit launched in 1980.
PHILOSOPHY This historically minded rum is produced to mirror the original Admiralty blend of the British Royal Navy.

The spirit Following tradition, this proper "Navy Rum" is distilled in wooden pot stills. The molasses comes from sugar cane grown in the Demerara River Valley, aka the "Valley of Navy Rum." The rum is aged for at least three years in charred oak bourbon barrels.

The taste This round yet smooth spirit smells of demerara, molasses, dried fruit, and spices, with a warm, long finish.

Revolte

Rum, 41.5% ABV

DISTILLERY Revolte Rum, Worms-Westhofen, Germany. Founded in 2015.
PHILOSOPHY Following its own path by using a self-cultivated yeast normally used for wines.

The spirit Using molasses imported from Papua New Guinea, the Master Distiller oversees every step in the production process to achieve a rum with distinctive character and a complex aroma.

The taste This rum's grape and banana aromas are completed by flavors of mature mango, plum, and raisin.

Rhum J.M Agricole

Rum, 50% ABV

DISTILLERY Distillerie Fonds-Preville, Macouba, Martinique. Spirit launched in 1845.
PHILOSOPHY Using sugar cane known for its terroir-driven character, this small producer makes rhum agricole at Martinique's oldest distillery.

The spirit Within an hour of being harvested from the side of a volcano, sugar cane is crushed. After it has been fermented, the wash is distilled through a copper column. After three months in stainless steel, the rhum is bottled.

The taste Bright aromas and flavors of fresh meringue, confectioners' sugar, cucumber, and cane stalk emanate from the liquid. The long finish features notes of pepper, sweet cream, and wet stone.

The family crest and flags have become the trademark for the boutique rhum distillery

The initials J.M stand for the original founder, Jean-Marie Martin

The illustration shows how the rhum was originally transported to market in Martinique's capital city, St. Pierre—full barrels would be floated out to sea, and then transported by boat

Richland Single Estate

Rum, 43% ABV

DISTILLERY Richland Distillery, Georgia, USA. Spirit launched in 2013.
PHILOSOPHY The first single-estate rum producer in America manually produces "field-to-glass" rum, made from its own sugar cane.

The spirit Freshly pressed, unrefined sugar-cane juice is fermented using a proprietary yeast, then run through a pot still just once. The rum is matured in virgin American oak, and after two to four years, select barrels are bottled.

The taste This spirit smells of vanilla, cinnamon, caramel, anise, honey, and toasted oak, and features flavor notes of chocolate, butterscotch, and clove.

Ron del Barrilito

Rum, 43% ABV

DISTILLERY Edmundo B. Fernández, Inc., Puerto Rico, USA. Spirit launched in 1880.
PHILOSOPHY One of the Caribbean's most famous names in rum strives to maintain the same quality and process since its origins in 1880.

The spirit To make its Ron del Barrilito ("rum from the little barrel"), the producer adheres to its closely guarded secret formula. Charred oak barrels are used for the aging process to impart a rich amber–gold hue.

The taste Smooth and mellow on the palate, this rum offers an interesting, smoky flavor that is best enjoyed straight or over ice.

These symbolize the medals obtained for quality in several Expositions in the US between 1901 and 1906

The P and F are the initials of the creator of Ron del Barrilito, engineer Pedro Fernández

Roaring Dan's

Rum, 45% ABV

DISTILLERY Great Lakes Distillery, Wisconsin, USA. Founded in 2010.
PHILOSOPHY Located in the heart of Milwaukee, this small-batch producer uses old-world methods and local ingredients.

The spirit This rum is named after the only man ever arrested for piracy on the Great Lakes. It is distilled from fermented sugar-cane molasses, and gets its sweetness from local maple syrup, which is added before the second distillation. The rum is aged in new charred American white oak barrels and used bourbon barrels.

The taste Full of character, there is a buttery sweetness on the palate thanks to the maple, followed by a dry finish.

Santa Teresa 1796

Rum, 40% ABV

DISTILLERY Ron Santa Teresa, Estado Aragua, Venezuela. Founded in 1796.
PHILOSOPHY This charitable producer's values of humility, pride, and transformation are expressed through its award-winning rums.

The spirit This sipping rum is produced using the Solera method, in which an array of light and dark rums—aged for 4–35 years in used bourbon barrels—are blended together and aged in a variety of barrels.

The taste Amber red in color, the spirit has a fruity aroma, with a silky mouthfeel and flavors of toasted wood, leather, and tobacco.

Rougaroux Sugarshine

Rum, 50.5% ABV

DISTILLERY Donner-Peltier Distillers, Louisiana, USA. Founded in 2012.
PHILOSOPHY Producing "cane-to-glass" rum using the freshest Louisiana-grown ingredients.

The spirit Named after the Cajun Country "bogeyman," this rum is made from a proprietary mix of locally sourced sugar and molasses. The staff ferments the mix for a week, then distills it in an 800-gallon (3,600-liter) copper pot still.

The taste This bold rum features an aggressive nose, similar to moonshine. Alcohol flavor notes are offset by hints of thick molasses and brown sugar.

Scarlet Ibis Trinidad

Rum, 49% ABV

DISTILLERY Angostura, Port of Spain, Trinidad. Spirit launched in 2009.
PHILOSOPHY Named after Trinidad's national bird, this cocktail-driven rum was initially commissioned by one of New York City's most acclaimed cocktail bars.

The spirit This product was created to appease bartenders who wanted a flavor-intense rum, versatile enough for multiple cocktail applications. After distillation occurs in a column still, a blend of rums are aged in used American oak for three to five years.

The taste Much drier compared to other rums from the region, this strong expression of the spirit carries notes of earth, tobacco, and toffee.

Smatt's Gold

Rum, 40% ABV

DISTILLERY Smatt's Distillery, Trelawny, Jamaica. Spirit launched in 2006.
PHILOSOPHY Dating back to the earliest days of rum production in the Caribbean, this distillery uses traditional processing methods.

The spirit This producer sources sugar cane from the naturally rich soil of the Smatt family estates. After fermentation with wild, local yeast, distillation occurs in copper pot stills and column stills. The rum is aged in used bourbon barrels.

The taste This creamy, spicy rum contains notes of demerara, toasted coconut, dried apricot, and mango.

Starr African

Rum, 40% ABV

DISTILLERY Starr, Flic-en-Flac, Mauritius. Founded in 1926.
PHILOSOPHY This rum is made entirely in Africa, using fair-labor, fair-trade, and eco-friendly techniques to preserve the pristine island environment.

The spirit This single-estate rum is grown, distilled, and aged on-site from its pristine island's much-coveted sugar cane. The finished product is a blend of rums aged up to six years in a variety of mature Scotch barrels.

The taste Smooth and clean, this rum sports flavors of cherry and cardamom, with hints of citrus, nutmeg, star anise, cinnamon, and vanilla.

HOW TO ENJOY
This is best enjoyed mixed in cocktails.

Smith & Cross

Rum, 57% ABV

DISTILLERY Hampden Estates, Trelawny, Jamaica. Spirit launched in 2010.
PHILOSOPHY Honoring the aromatic style that made Jamaican rum the cornerstone of many classic cocktails.

The spirit Sugar-cane molasses ferments in old wood vats and dunder pits (dunder is the liquid left in a boiler after distilling a batch of rum). It is distilled in an old pot still.

The taste This strong-flavored rum offers notes of bread, flambéed bananas, and tobacco.

Vizcaya VXOP

Rum, 40% ABV

DISTILLERY Oliver & Oliver, Santo Domingo, Dominican Republic. Founded in 1982.
PHILOSOPHY One of the Caribbean's most award-winning rums is proud to use the Cuban-style "Guarapo" method, in which fresh sugar-cane juice is used rather than molasses.

The spirit This handcrafted rum is a blend of various rums distilled from sugar-cane juice and aged in bourbon barrels. Each batch is personally tasted and approved by the producer.

The taste This spicy rum offers ginger, nutmeg, and cinnamon on the nose and vanilla, honey, and caramel on the palate.

HOW TO ENJOY
This is perfect straight, or over ice.

Three Sheets

Rum, 40% ABV

DISTILLERY Ballast Point Brewing and Spirits, California, USA. Founded in 2008.
PHILOSOPHY What began as a small home-brew supply shop has grown into a successful craft brewery and distillery—the first in San Diego post-Prohibition.

The spirit Known for its innovative approach, this producer uses a hybrid pot-and-column still to create a smooth silver rum. Pure sugar cane is used for distinctive fermentation characteristics.

The taste This light, clean-tasting rum carries sweetness from the sugar cane. Aromas of pineapple, dulce de leche, and caramel delight the nose.

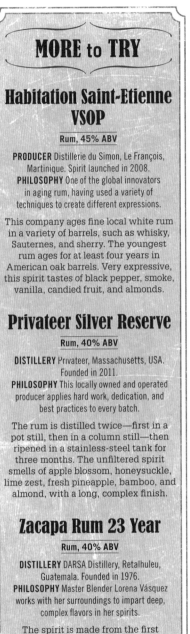

MORE to TRY

Habitation Saint-Etienne VSOP

Rum, 45% ABV

PRODUCER Distillerie du Simon, Le François, Martinique. Spirit launched in 2008.
PHILOSOPHY One of the global innovators in aging rum, having used a variety of techniques to create different expressions.

This company ages fine local white rum in a variety of barrels, such as whisky, Sauternes, and sherry. The youngest rum ages for at least four years in American oak barrels. Very expressive, this spirit tastes of black pepper, smoke, vanilla, candied fruit, and almonds.

Privateer Silver Reserve

Rum, 40% ABV

DISTILLERY Privateer, Massachusetts, USA. Founded in 2011.
PHILOSOPHY This locally owned and operated producer applies hard work, dedication, and best practices to every batch.

The rum is distilled twice—first in a pot still, then in a column still—then ripened in a stainless-steel tank for three months. The unfiltered spirit smells of apple blossom, honeysuckle, lime zest, fresh pineapple, bamboo, and almond, with a long, complex finish.

Zacapa Rum 23 Year

Rum, 40% ABV

DISTILLERY DARSA Distillery, Retalhuleu, Guatemala. Founded in 1976.
PHILOSOPHY Master Blender Lorena Vásquez works with her surroundings to impart deep, complex flavors in her spirits.

The spirit is made from the first pressing of virgin sugar-cane honey. The rum is Solera-aged, 7,500 feet (2,300 meters) above sea level, to smooth the process. Intense and woody on the nose, this rum includes notes of vanilla, caramel, and chocolate.

Infusing Rum

Sweet, spicy, and tropical, most rums respond well to complementary infusions, which can improve rum-based, tropical cocktails such as the Mai Tai. Lighter, younger rums are better at picking up the infusion's flavors. For best results, follow the instructions on pages 24–25.

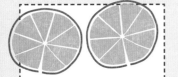

Blood Orange

Give your rum a touch of the complex, sweet–tart flavor of blood orange.

What you need
2 blood oranges, peeled and cut into wheels; 3 cups rum.

Infusing time 3–5 days.

The next level Add ½ vanilla pod into the infusion to temper the acidity of the citrus.

Cinnamon–Clove

Ramp up rum's herbal flavors by infusing it with spiced cloves and cinnamon.

What you need ½ tsp dried cloves; 2 cinnamon sticks; 3 cups rum.

Infusing time 2–3 days.

The next level Add ½ tsp allspice or one vanilla pod into the infusion for added complexity.

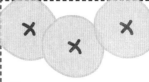

Banana

Infusing with banana gives a rich, creamy rum that is perfect for tropical drinks.

What you need 2 ripe bananas, cut into chunks; 3 cups rum.

Infusing time 1–2 weeks.

The next level You can add 1–2 tbsp dried coconut (or coconut juice) to the infusion to heighten the tropical experience.

Habanero

Add spice but beware— fiery habaneros will overwhelm an infusion if left for too long.

What you need
1–2 habanero peppers, seeded and sliced; 3 cups rum.

Infusing time
12–24 hours.

The next level Counterbalance the habanero's considerable heat by adding in 1–2 tbsp honey or agave syrup.

Pineapple

Sweet, tropical pineapple creates a classic infusion for any rum.

What you need
1 pineapple, peeled and cut into chunks; 3 cups rum.

Infusing time 5–7 days.

The next level To heighten rum's spicy notes, add a 1-in (2.5-cm) piece fresh ginger, peeled and thinly sliced.

Mango

Fresh mango is difficult to prepare, but it rewards the effort thanks to the sweet, tropical flavor it brings to rum.

What you need 1 mango, peeled, sliced, and pitted; 3 cups rum.

Infusing time 5–7 days.

The next level Slice a jalapeño pepper and add the slices to the infusion to add spice and temper the mango's natural sugars.

Daiquiri

The Daiquiri, the world's favorite rum cocktail, originated 100 years ago from the town of the same name in Cuba. Elegant and refined, it garnered international champions such as Ernest Hemingway, whose Cuban exploits were legendary. Avoid today's mass-produced frozen versions and create variations using the delicate classic as a starting point.

The Classic Recipe

The Daiquiri is a simple mixture of rum, lime, and sugar, served ultra-cold.

1 Pour 2fl oz (60ml) light rum into a shaker.
2 Pour in 1fl oz (30ml) fresh lime juice.
3 Add 1 tablespoon simple syrup.
4 Fill with ice cubes, shake hard for 10 seconds, then strain into a chilled coupe glass. Serve.

Create Your Own Signature Mix

Key Components

1 Pour **2fl oz (60ml) light rum** into a shaker.

This cocktail is the perfect vessel for any rum—you could replace light rum with an intense agricole rum or a spiced Jamaican version.

2 Pour in **1fl oz (30ml) fresh lime juice**.

Fresh lime juice provides a tart counterpoint to the cocktail's other sweet ingredients. If lime is not your thing, try an alternative such as grapefruit (Hemingway's favorite) or lemon.

3 Add **1 tablespoon simple syrup**.

Simple syrup is the standard sugar component, but you could try sweetened lime syrup or limeade.

4 Fill with **ice cubes**, shake hard for 10 seconds, and strain into your glass.

For extra-cold or less-potent results, allow some ice to escape from the shaker, or add crushed ice to the glass.

Simple syrup

Lime juice

Rum

Additional Flourishes

Garnish Coat the rim—vanilla-scented sugar is a pretty and tasty option—or garnish with some dehydrated tropical fruit.

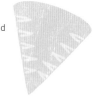

Infuse Flavor your own simple syrup, using anything from fresh mint to vanilla beans to add an extra hit of flavor (see p27).

Craft Reinventions

Bartenders around the world reinvent the Daiquiri all the time. Many keep it simple and experiment with a range of rums and fruit accents of flavor—just like these three innovative and exciting variations.

Jamaican Daiquiri

Pour the liquid ingredients into a shaker. Add ice cubes and shake hard for 10 seconds. Strain into a chilled coupe glass. Garnish with nutmeg and a slice of orange, and serve.

slice of orange
grated nutmeg
1 tbsp simple syrup
1 tbsp fresh lime juice
1 tbsp allspice liqueur
3fl oz (90ml) Jamaican rum

Hipster Hemingway

Pour the liquid ingredients into a shaker. Add ice cubes and shake hard for 10 seconds. Strain into a chilled coupe glass. Garnish with the cherry and grapefruit, and serve.

dehydrated slice of grapefruit
rum-soaked cherry
1fl oz (30ml) fresh grapefruit juice
1 tbsp fresh lime juice
1 tbsp maraschino liqueur
2fl oz (60ml) agricole rum

◀ Coconut–Pineapple Daiquiri

Pour the liquid ingredients into a shaker. Add ice cubes and shake hard for 10 seconds. Strain into a chilled coupe glass. Garnish with the rose petals and coconut, and serve.

ribbons of coconut
crystallized yellow rose petals
1 tbsp fresh lemon juice
1 tbsp fresh pineapple juice
1 tbsp coconut milk
2fl oz (60ml) light rum

Hurricane

The Hurricane is the perfect choice for those who love all things sweet. Bright red in color, it is synonymous with Mardi Gras parties and one of New Orleans' most famous bars, Pat O'Brien's. Year-round, scores of visitors sway down Bourbon Street with the drink's iconic glass. For a festive time, play around with the recipe to find your favorite.

The Classic Recipe

Serve this sweet cocktail in a hurricane glass if you like, although a collins glass gives the same result.

1 Pour 1½fl oz (45ml) each dark rum and light rum into a shaker.

2 Add 1fl oz (30ml) fresh lime juice and ¾fl oz (20ml) fresh orange juice.

3 Add 1fl oz (30ml) passionfruit syrup and 1 tablespoon each simple syrup and grenadine.

4 Add ice cubes, and shake for 10 seconds. Strain into an ice-filled hurricane or collins glass.

Serve it up Garnish with an orange slice and maraschino cherry.

Create Your Own Signature Mix

Key Components

1 Pour **1½fl oz (45ml) each dark rum and light rum** into a shaker.

The classic is packed with rum. Most recipes use simple rums, but instead of a dark variety, try incorporating a spiced classic rum for complexity.

2 Add **1fl oz (30ml) fresh lime juice** and ¾fl oz (20ml) fresh **orange juice**.

These give a fresh fruit flavor—you can up the volume of citrus fruit juices for increased sourness, or use pineapple juice to yield a mellow–sweet profile.

3 Add **1fl oz (30ml) passionfruit syrup** and **1 tablespoon each simple syrup and grenadine**.

Syrups give a sweet profile and the iconic red color. You could also use puréed fruit, such as strawberries.

4 Add **ice cubes**, and shake for 10 seconds. Strain into an **ice-filled** glass.

It is best to use ice cubes, although crushed ice helps to dilute the sweetness. For fruity ice cubes, drop passionfruit pulp or orange juice into the water before freezing.

Ice cubes

Syrups

Fruit juices

Rum

Additional Flourishes

Garnish Serve your Daiquiri with blood orange, pineapple, or grapefruit slices to complement the drink.

Berries Add a boozy kick by soaking fresh cherries in dark rum or liqueur for a couple of hours. Pop them in the glass with the ice.

Decorate For a chic, festive touch, you could decorate the drink with bright-colored edible flowers, such as pansies, violas, or marigolds.

Craft Reinventions

A Hurricane without gale-force sweetness just isn't a Hurricane, but there are steps bartenders take—such as adding fresh passionfruit or soda water—to yield a more balanced drink. Follow their lead with these variations.

Fizzy Hurricane

Shake the light rum, liqueur, soda, bitters, juices, and ice in a shaker for 10 seconds. Strain into an ice-filled collins glass. Over the back of a spoon, pour in the overproof rum. Top with fruit. Serve.

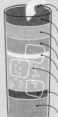

- slice of lemon and a maraschino cherry
- 1fl oz (30ml) overproof rum
- 1fl oz (30ml) fresh lime juice
- 1fl oz (30ml) fresh orange juice
- dash of lemon bitters
- 4fl oz (120ml) soda
- 1 tbsp maraschino liqueur
- 2fl oz (60ml) light rum

Blood Orange Hurricane

Pour the rums, syrup, bitters, and juices into a shaker. Add ice cubes, and shake for 10 seconds. Strain into an ice-filled collins glass. Garnish with the slice of blood orange, and serve.

- dehydrated slice of blood orange
- 1½fl oz (45ml) fresh blood orange juice
- 1fl oz (30ml) fresh lime juice
- dash of spiced bitters
- 1 tbsp agave syrup
- 1½fl oz (45ml) light rum
- 1½fl oz (45ml) agricole rum

◄ Passionfruit Hurricane

Pour the rums, bitters, pulp, sugar, and juice into a shaker. Add ice, and shake for 10 seconds. Strain into a collins glass filled with crushed ice. Top with the passionfruit, and serve.

- half a passionfruit
- 1fl oz (30ml) fresh lime juice
- 1 tbsp superfine sugar
- 1½fl oz (45ml) fresh passionfruit pulp
- dash of orange bitters
- 1½fl oz (45ml) light rum
- 1½fl oz (45ml) dark rum

Mojito

The Mojito is Cuba's most popular contribution to the global bar scene. More labor-intensive than most cocktails, it is often blamed for "muddler's elbow." The lime and mint are the perfect counterbalance to the rum, creating what many consider as the ideal tropical cocktail. Splash, shake, and muddle your way to refreshing variations.

The Classic Recipe

This traditional Cuban highball uses less rum than other similar cocktails.

1 Place 2 tablespoons granulated sugar into a collins glass.

2 Add 8 mint leaves.

3 Pour in 1fl oz (30ml) soda and gently muddle to release essential oils.

4 Slice one medium lime into quarters. Squeeze the quarters into your glass and drop two into the glass.

5 Fill the glass with ice cubes.

6 Pour in 2fl oz (60ml) light rum. Gently stir and top up with soda.

Serve it up Garnish with a sprig of mint.

Create Your Own Signature Mix

Key Components

1 Place **2 tablespoons granulated sugar** into your glass.

Try brown sugar for a richer sweetness; natural agave syrup also blends well.

2 Add **8 mint leaves**.

Fresh mint yields best results. Seek out different kinds of mint—spearmint, lavender mint, or Moroccan mint can add new herbal notes.

3 Pour in **1fl oz (30ml) soda** and muddle.

You can make lemon- or lime-infused soda, or try spicy ginger beer.

4 Slice **one medium lime** into quarters. Squeeze the quarters into your glass and drop two into the glass.

Lime quarters provide the most flavor, but fresh lime juice also works.

5 Fill the glass with **ice cubes**.

Kick up the drink's mint quota by freezing chopped mint with water.

6 Pour in **2fl oz (60ml) light rum**, stir, and top up with **soda**.

Light rum complements the other ingredients. For a deeper flavor, use half dark and half light rum.

Ice cubes

Soda

Rum

Lime

Mint and soda

Sugar

Additional Flourishes

Garnish A slice of dried ginger or pieces of crystallized ginger nicely complements the drink's flavors. Or try a slice of dehydrated lime for an offbeat decoration.

Fruit Muddle or purée fresh fruit with the mint, sugar, and lime. Whole raspberries and lightly puréed watermelon are both great choices.

Craft Reinventions

There are hundreds of variations around the globe. Many use unusual ingredients, such as calamansi citrus fruit or yerba buena mint. These innovative recipes (see right) start with the cocktail's versatile base and introduce new flavors.

Ginger Mojito

Gently muddle the mint leaves, juice, and simple syrup in a collins glass. Add ice cubes and the rum, and gently stir. Top up with ginger beer, garnish with the mint and ginger, and serve.

- fresh mint and crystallized ginger
- ginger beer
- 2fl oz (60ml) light rum
- 1 tbsp ginger-infused simple syrup
- 1½fl oz (45ml) fresh lime juice
- 8 mint leaves

Spiced Pear Mojito

Gently muddle the mint leaves, juice, purée, bitters, and sugar in a collins glass. Add ice cubes and the rums, and gently stir. Top up with soda, garnish with pear, lime, and mint, and serve.

- fresh mint and a wedge of lime
- slice of pear
- soda
- 1fl oz (30ml) each of light and dark rum
- 2 tbsp brown sugar
- dash of mint bitters
- 1fl oz (30ml) pear purée
- 1fl oz (30ml) fresh lime juice
- 6 mint leaves

◄ Matcha Tea Mojito

Gently muddle the mint leaves, juice, and simple syrup in a collins glass. Add ice cubes, then pour in the rum and Matcha tea, and gently stir. Garnish with the mint, and serve.

- fresh mint
- 2½fl oz (75ml) cold water, whisked with ½ tsp Matcha
- 1½fl oz (45ml) light rum
- 1fl oz (30ml) simple syrup
- 1fl oz (30ml) fresh lime juice
- 8 mint leaves

Rum and Ginger

The Rum and Ginger, also known as a Dark and Stormy, was first served more than 100 years ago. It hails from the tropical island of Bermuda. Techniques and ratios vary, but the classic requires only two ingredients and offers the perfect flavor profile for savoring dark rum. Create an intense and stormy drink that is worthy of a Caribbean paradise.

The Classic Recipe

Darker than most, this is the easiest rum cocktail to master.

1 Fill a collins glass with ice.
2 Add 2fl oz (60ml) dark rum.
3 Top up with ginger beer. Stir (if desired).
4 Top with a wedge of lime, and serve.

Create Your Own Signature Mix

Key Components

1 Fill a collins glass with **ice cubes**.
For added flavor, mix a little grated ginger or lime juice in water before freezing, or opt for crushed ice for a slushier mouthfeel.

2 Add **2fl oz (60ml) dark rum**.
The classic calls for Bermuda's native rum, but any dark rum should work. Agricole rhums provide a fun flavor-rich alternative. If you are new to rum, start with a light rum or try a 50:50 mix of light and dark.

3 Top up with **ginger beer**.
Stir (if desired).
Use crisp, top-quality ginger beer rather than sugary-sweet ginger ale. For a true craft effect, make your own ginger syrup and combine it with soda water.

4 Top with a **wedge of lime**.
This is a vital garnish—drinkers can squeeze as much juice as they like into the drink.

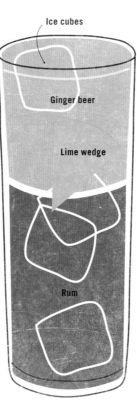

Ice cubes

Ginger beer

Lime wedge

Rum

Additional Flourishes

Shake You may prefer to shake the rum with around 1fl oz (30ml) fresh lime juice. Pour it over ice and top up with ginger beer.

Infuse You can also infuse the rum for two days with spices and fruit such as freshly ground cloves, black and pink peppercorns, allspice, nutmeg, cinnamon, and orange zest.

Heat Chile-lovers could gently muddle one seeded and finely chopped red chile pepper with two ice cubes and a wedge of lime. Pour the rum and ginger beer over the top, and serve.

Craft Reinventions

A Rum and Ginger is the ideal platform for experimenting with home infusions. Mixologists start with dark rum, add their favorite fruits and spices, and have fun with the results. Give these three modern variations a whirl.

Dark and Spicy

Fill a collins glass with ice, add the rum and bitters, and gently stir. Top up with ginger beer. Garnish with a wedge of lime and cinnamon stick, and serve.

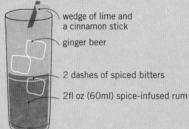

- wedge of lime and a cinnamon stick
- ginger beer
- 2 dashes of spiced bitters
- 2fl oz (60ml) spice-infused rum

Extra Dark and Stormy

Fill a collins glass with ice, add the overproof rum, syrup, and bitters, and gently stir. Top up with ginger beer. Garnish with a wedge of lime and crystallized ginger, and serve.

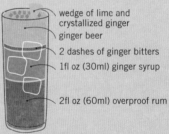

- wedge of lime and crystallized ginger
- ginger beer
- 2 dashes of ginger bitters
- 1fl oz (30ml) ginger syrup
- 2fl oz (60ml) overproof rum

◀ Cranberry Storm

Fill a collins glass with ice, add the rum and bitters, and gently stir. Top up with ginger beer. Garnish with the cranberries and a wedge of orange, and serve.

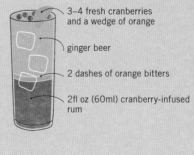

- 3–4 fresh cranberries and a wedge of orange
- ginger beer
- 2 dashes of orange bitters
- 2fl oz (60ml) cranberry-infused rum

Mai Tai

The Mai Tai is the most famous of all tiki drinks, and can be traced back to the beach bars of 1940s California. Sweet and fruity, this is the taste of the tropics. Often served in a colorful tiki mug, the drink received its name from *Maita'i*, the Tahitian word for "good." Adapt it your way—you could embrace kitsch cocktail decorations or try a chic alternative.

The Classic Recipe

This is devilishly easy to consume, thanks to its sweet flavor. It is tradionally served in a tiki mug.

1 Pour 2fl oz (60ml) dark rum into a shaker.

2 Add 1fl oz (30ml) fresh lime juice.

3 Add 1 tablespoon each orange liqueur and orgeat syrup and 2 teaspoons simple syrup.

4 Shake for 10 seconds, then strain into an ice-filled double old-fashioned glass or tiki mug.

Serve it up Garnish with a skewer of pineapple chunks, cherry, and mint.

Create Your Own Signature Mix

Key Components

1 Pour **2fl oz (60ml) dark rum** into a shaker.

Rum-packed Mai Tais often call for spiced Jamaican rum, but you may find a gentler white rum appealing. Try a mix of light and dark rums to discover a good balance of flavors.

2 Add **1fl oz (30ml) fresh lime juice**.

Fresh lime juice helps to cut through the drink's sweetness. Try fresh grapefruit juice as an alternative.

3 Add **1 tablespoon each orange liqueur and orgeat syrup** and **2 teaspoons simple syrup**.

These ingredients combine to create the sweet flavor. Tropical fruits suit this cocktail, so you could try pineapple-based liqueur instead of orange. A dash or two of almond extract or a tablespoon almond liqueur can replace orgeat syrup.

4 Shake for 10 seconds, then strain into an **ice-filled** glass or mug.

Cubes are the classic choice, but you could also try pouring the cocktail over crushed ice for a slushy-style result.

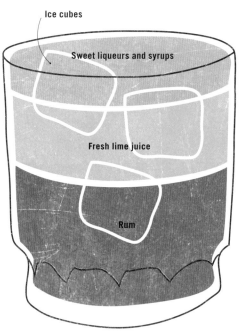

Ice cubes

Sweet liqueurs and syrups

Fresh lime juice

Rum

Additional Flourishes

Bitters You can now buy sweet Tiki bitters to suit tropical cocktails. If you prefer, add a dash of citrus bitters for added sharpness.

Decorate Pick up on the tropical flavors of the drink with eye-catching pineapple-leaf decorations.

Garnish This cocktail suits show-stopping garnishes. Go wild with skewers, umbrellas, and plastic toys.

Craft Reinventions

The king of tiki cocktails, the Mai Tai is ripe for reinvention. As it is so sweet, mixologists often play with sour or bitter notes of flavor to give it a new profile. Give this classic a new spin with the three variation recipes on the right.

Bitter Mai Tai

Shake the rum, Campari, liqueur, lime juice, syrup, and ice in a shaker for 10 seconds. Strain into an ice-filled double old-fashioned glass. Add bitters, top with skewered cherries, and serve.

- 2 maraschino cherries
- 2 dashes Angostura bitters
- 1 tbsp orgeat syrup
- 1fl oz (30ml) lime juice
- 1 tbsp orange liqueur
- 1¾fl oz (50ml) Campari
- 1fl oz (30ml) dark rum

Coconut Pineapple Mai Tai

Shake the rums, liqueur, juices, coconut milk, syrup, and ice in a shaker for 10 seconds. Strain into an ice-filled double old-fashioned glass. Garnish with the fruit, and serve.

- 2 maraschino cherries and 2 pineapple chunks
- 1 tbsp orgeat syrup
- ¾fl oz (20ml) fresh coconut milk
- 1 tbsp lime juice
- 1 tbsp pineapple juice
- 1 tbsp orange liqueur
- 1fl oz (30ml) each of dark and light rum

◀ Bloody Mai Tai

Shake the rums, liqueur, juice, syrup, and ice in a shaker for 10 seconds. Strain into an ice-filled double old-fashioned glass. Pour in the grenadine and bitters. Top with the peel, and serve.

- skewered orange peel
- 3 dashes Angostura bitters
- 1 tbsp grenadine
- 1 tbsp orgeat syrup
- 1fl oz (30ml) lime juice
- 1 tbsp orange liqueur
- 1fl oz (30ml) each of dark and light rum

Brandy—from the Dutch word *brandewijn* ("burned wine")—is made by **distilling** rudimentary fruit **wine**. Most brandies are aged in wooden barrels, sometimes with added colors and flavors. The best are held for decades to achieve incredible **depths of flavor**. Fine brandies, and the French expressions from Cognac and Armagnac, were once thought of as old-fashioned after-dinner drinks, but forward-thinking producers have brought them into the twenty-first century, using **unusual fruit bases** and returning to artisanal techniques. Pisco from Peru and Chile, plus clear fruit brandies—known as eau-de-vies—have changed the way the world thinks about unaged fruit spirits. Find out what **the buzz** is about and discover how a craft brandy can **elevate your cocktails** to the next level.

BRANDY
AND COGNAC

BarSol Quebranta

Pisco, 40% ABV

DISTILLERY Bodega San Isidro, Pueblo Nuevo, Peru. Founded in 1919.
PHILOSOPHY This producer is bringing quality pisco from Peru to bars around the world.

The spirit Distilled in a copper pot still, this traditional pisco puro (grape brandy) is made from fully fermented must, which is freshly pressed grape juice that contains the skins, seeds, and stems.

The taste Subtle aromas and flavors of hay, banana, and ripe dark berry delight the senses, with a long and elegant finish.

Castarède VSOP

Armagnac, 40% ABV

DISTILLERY Armagnac Castarède, Gascony, France. Founded in 1832.
PHILOSOPHY This is the oldest Armagnac trading house in France. It takes a dynamic approach to developing its spirits while maintaining a respect for the environment.

The spirit Produced in a sustainable and eco-friendly fashion, this is a blend of Armagnacs that are all at least eight years old and made from local Gascony wine that has been single-distilled in a continuous still. The blend is aged for at least five years in oak casks.

The taste Amber and spicy, this intense spirit carries notes of pepper, coconut, walnut, and honey.

Christian Drouin Sélection

Calvados, 40% ABV

DISTILLERY Christian Drouin, Normandy, France. Founded in 1960.
PHILOSOPHY This traditional producer strives for quality and is committed to changing the international perception of Calvados.

The spirit Made from apples and pears from the Domfront region in northwest France, this spirit is distilled using a column still. The team matures the spirit in a diverse range of previously used barrels, which are mostly reconditioned Bordeaux barrels.

The taste Lighter in style than most Calvados, this spirit has remarkable fresh fruit flavor notes.

HOW TO ENJOY This Calvados is exceptional in cocktails.

Delamain Pale & Dry XO

Cognac, 40% ABV

PRODUCER Delamain, Cognac, France. Founded in 1824.
PHILOSOPHY One of the oldest Cognac producers, Delamain aims to deliver the purest, most authentic expression of the Grande Champagne area of Cognac.

The spirit Young eau de vie is purchased from grower–distillers, then aged separately in 75-gallon (350-liter) oak barrels. After 20–25 years of aging, the Cognac is blended, then allowed to age for an additional two years to marry the flavors and textures.

The taste Bright amber in color, this spirit gets its name from its natural color and level of sweetness, with notes of dried fruits and vanilla.

Domaine d'Esperance Folle-Blanche

Armagnac, 49% ABV

DISTILLERY Domaine d'Esperance, Gascony, France. Spirit launched in 2014.
PHILOSOPHY This traditional producer believes that love and care in the production process is the key to the best Armagnacs.

The spirit The producer distills the spirit at a very low temperature in a continuous still, which better preserves the grape aromas. The spirit is then poured into new oak barrels, before being aged in casks.

The taste This Armagnac features fruity notes of vanilla, wood, and licorice that come from the barrel-aging process.

Clear Creek Pear

Brandy, 40% ABV

DISTILLERY Clear Creek Distillery, Oregon, USA. Founded in 1985.
PHILOSOPHY One of America's foremost craft distilleries is renowned for its use of locally sourced fruit and European techniques.

The spirit Hood River-grown Bartlett pears are crushed, fermented, and distilled once in German-made copper pot stills. The only ingredients are pears—30lb (14kg) go into each bottle—and fresh reservoir water.

The taste From the intense nose and pure flavor to the clean aftertaste, sweet pear dominates the senses.

Domaine du Tariquet XO

Armagnac, 40% ABV

DISTILLERY Château du Tariquet, Gascony, France. Founded in 1912.
PHILOSOPHY This historic French producer's goal is to create Armagnacs that serve as a pure expression of the terroir where they are born.

The spirit Production begins with white wine grapes that are grown, pressed, and vinified on the estate. Tariquet favors single continuous-distillation in a traditional copper pot still, and ages the spirit in lightly toasted French oak barrels for 12–15 years.

The taste Rich and complex, this spirit pleases the eye with its amber–yellow hue. The powerful bouquet is dominated by almonds and quince, and you can recognize notes of prunes and toasted nuts.

Encanto

Pisco, 40.5% ABV

DISTILLERY Campo de Encanto, Ica, Peru. Founded in 2010.
PHILOSOPHY This handcrafted, artisanal pisco was created by a bartender, sommelier, and distiller—together they keep the production as close to the terroir as possible.

The spirit Strictly following the DOC guidelines for making pisco in Peru, the producers use hand-harvested grapes from single vineyards. The fruit undergoes a one- to two-week fermentation, then distillation in a copper pot. After resting for a year, the spirit is blended.

The taste This vibrant, pure grape spirit offers a smooth texture and bright aromas, with tastes of cinnamon, stone fruits, menthol, almonds, and lavender.

Germain-Robin Select Barrel XO

Brandy, 40% ABV

DISTILLERY Germain-Robin, California, USA. Founded in 1982.
PHILOSOPHY With a heritage of distilling and cellaring expertise, this producer blazed new trails by distilling premium wine-grape varietals instead of the neutral grapes of Cognac.

The spirit This spirit is assembled from 12 different varietal brandies of a similar age, seven of them pinot noirs (80 percent of the volume). Aging occurs in air-dried limousin oak, and to achieve the final product, the team reduces the proof with filtered rainwater. Only 10 barrels per year are produced.

The taste The use of pinot noir grapes in its composition explains this brandy's distinctively soft richness. It has a long and complex finish.

H by HINE VSOP

Cognac, 40% ABV

PRODUCER HINE, Cognac, France. Founded in 1817.

PHILOSOPHY In response to a growing demand for a cocktail-friendly Cognac, the Cellar Master Eric Forget collaborated with the French Bartenders Association to create H by HINE.

The spirit This spirit is a harmonious blend of 20 Cognacs made from grapes grown in the Grande Champagne and Petite Champagne regions, all aged for at least four years.

The taste Deep amber in color, this young Cognac carries soft aromas of toffee and raisins. The silky mouthfeel transitions into tastes of peppery spice, fruit, and nuts.

Grosperrin XO Fine Champagne

Cognac, 42.5% ABV

PRODUCER La Gabare, Cognac Grosperrin, Saintes, France. Founded in 1992.

PHILOSOPHY One of the last independent Cognac houses was founded by Jean Grosperrin. His son, Guilhem, runs the house and continues to work with a network of growers.

The spirit Batches from individual growers are left in their original barrels until the final blend or "coupe." The XO is a blend of more than 100 different Cognacs, including a Petite Champagne from 1969.

The taste Zesty and balanced, this complex spirit carries concentrated notes of sweet citrus, raisins, and fragrant white grapes.

Laird's Straight Apple

Brandy, 50% ABV

DISTILLERY Laird & Company, Virginia, USA. Founded in 1780.

PHILOSOPHY This producer prizes its heritage—the Lairds are the oldest family of distillers in the USA, now on their eighth and ninth generations.

The spirit The team washes, grinds, and presses ripe apples. The juice ferments for approximately one week to make a fermented cider. This liquid is distilled and then aged in charred, once-used oak barrels for a minimum of three years.

The taste Honey brown in color, this brandy offers a bright apple aroma with spicy notes. On the tongue, caramel and peppery spice yield to a tart finish.

Grosperrin XO Fine Champagne is produced by Cognac Grosperrin, a family-run Cognac house based in Saintes, in the Poitou-Charente region of France. It is a single-vintage Cognac of rare quality, crafted from grapes from the Cognac *crus* (growing regions), decades of careful storage, and the blending expertise of the La Gabare cellar masters.

What's the story?

Jean Grosperrin developed a keen nose for excellent Cognacs while working first as a local broker for wine growers, and then later as a wholesaler mediating between merchants and growers. Wine-growing families often retain a few barrels of the fruits of each harvest for themselves—Jean realized that this treasure trove of ancient Cognacs was almost inaccessible to anyone from the outside world. Using his contacts and expertise, he began to purchase the finest of these vintages—storing, bottling, and sometimes blending them—and founded La Gabare in 1992. Today, his work is continued by his son, Guilhem.

The Grosperrin vintages demonstrate the great differences between the six terroirs of Cognac, from the Grande Champagne to the Bois Ordinaires. Each vintage has its own distinctive personality, celebrated in both the single-vintage bottles and the blends. There are strict rules governing ingredients, locale, and traceability: in order to be classified as a vintage with *Appellation d'Origine Contrôlée* or "AOP" (protected designation of origin), sellers must have detailed documentation of each cask's journey from vineyard to bottle.

Right This worker is training to be a Master Blender. Here, he bottles a very old batch of Cognac Grosperrin.

WINNERS of four GOLD medals at the Global Cognac Masters in 2015

There are

81,500

bottles' worth of vintage **Cognac** in the cellars

Most **Grosperrin vintages** exist in quantities of **less than 110 gallons** (500 liters)

Who is behind it?

Guilhem Grosperrin (below, right) took over the family business in 2003. Like his father, Grosperrin is keen to make and blend Cognac in the most natural way, without the addition of sugar or caramel. Guilhem's sister, **Axelle Grosperrin** (below, left), runs the wine and spirit shop next to the family's cellar in Saintes, France.

Above A worker prepares a batch of 1982 Fins Bois. Every bottle is labeled by hand.

Left Guilhem Grosperrin in the "laboratory," sampling vintages from the extensive Grosperrin cellars.

Larressingle VSOP

Armagnac, 40% ABV

DISTILLERY Château de Larressingle, Gascony, France. Founded in 1837.
PHILOSOPHY One of the very few Armagnac producers still owned by the founding family, Larressingle marries generations of tradition, respect for the terroir, and the advantages of modern-distillation technology.

The spirit Blended from spirits originating in Armagnac's two highest-quality growing regions—Bas Armagnac and Ténarèze—this spirit is made from a base wine that the producers distill in a small pot still, then age in the traditional oak casks, and finally blend.

The taste Supple with lots of fruit, the liquid yields a rich bouquet of prunes and a lingering, mellow finish.

Osocalis XO

Brandy, 40% ABV

DISTILLERY Osocalis Distillery, California, USA. Spirit launched in 2003.
PHILOSOPHY Osocalis creates spirits that combine Old World techniques with New World fruit.

The spirit Mirroring traditional Cognac production techniques, a two-stage distillation takes place in a pot still. Aging occurs for several years in carefully selected oak casks. During blending, the brandies marry in casks.

The taste This delicate brandy provides concentrated bursts of citrus, ginger, and caramel, with a long, rich finish.

Poire (Metté)

Eau de vie, 42% ABV

DISTILLERY Distillerie Metté, Alsace, France. Founded in 1960.
PHILOSOPHY One of France's most acclaimed brandy producers adheres to artisanal practices to create special spirits.

The spirit The producer carefully distills this eau de vie twice in very small copper pot stills. A total of 18–20lb (9–10kg) of pears from the Rhône Valley go into each bottle, without the need for artificial flavorings, colorings, or sugar.

The taste Pure and clean on the nose, notes of juicy pear carry throughout the tasting experience, with a silky mouthfeel and long-lasting finish.

Purkhart Blume Marillen

Eau de vie, 40% ABV

DISTILLERY Destillerie Purkhart, Steyr, Austria. Founded in 1931.
PHILOSOPHY This Austrian producer creates full-flavored, fruit-packed brandies in a style common to the Alps.

The spirit Double-distilled in traditional pot stills, this appropriately named product—translating as "blossom of the apricot"—captures the characteristics of Austria's prized Klosterneuburger apricot. Nearly 5lb (2.25kg) of the fruit goes into every bottle.

The taste Smooth and without burn in the finish, this spirit delivers the aromas of the apricot skins up front, and the flavors in the finish.

Portón

Pisco, 43% ABV

DISTILLERY Hacienda La Caravedo, Ica, Peru. Founded in 1684.
PHILOSOPHY Based at the oldest distillery in the Americas, this Peruvian producer uses centuries-old artisanal methods to handcraft the finest piscos.

The spirit This pisco is a blend of four different types of grapes, which are harvested by hand. The grapes ferment for 7–10 days in stainless steel, and distillation occurs in small batches in copper pot stills. The spirit rests in cement containers for at least a year before bottling.

The taste Crystal clear with medium viscosity, this full-bodied pisco presents flavors of cinnamon, orange blossom, and citrus.

Purkhart Pear Williams

Eau de vie, 40% ABV

DISTILLERY Destillerie Purkhart, Steyr, Austria. Founded in 1931.
PHILOSOPHY This Austrian producer creates full-flavored, fruit-packed brandies in a style common to the Alps.

The spirit This brandy contains a single variety of pears—Williams pears, grown in South Tirol. After the pears are fermented, the mash undergoes a single distillation in a pot still. Unlike most European brandies, water is the only additional ingredient to the distillate.

The taste This rich, creamy, and balanced brandy is aromatic of ripe pear skin, with a long, pear-packed finish.

St. George Pear

Brandy, 40% ABV

DISTILLERY St. George Spirits, California, USA. Founded in 1982.

PHILOSOPHY Founder Jörg Rupf (a trailblazer in the American craft spirits movement) established St. George Spirits to make exquisite New World brandies using Old World distillation techniques. Rupf's exacting standards continue to influence every spirit.

The spirit Organic, dry-farmed Bartlett pears are crushed at the peak of ripeness and then cold-fermented for about two weeks before being distilled in copper pot stills. Around 30lb (14kg) of fruit goes into every bottle.

The taste Fruit-forward and wildly aromatic on the nose, this dry brandy tastes of ripe Bartlett pears, with subtle honey notes and a hint of spice.

This pear was illustrated by Patricia Curtan, an artist best known for the iconic menus and cookbooks of the famous Chez Panisse restaurant, in Berkeley, California

The signatures of Jörg Rupf (founder) and Lance Winters (distiller) appear as part of the label design

Soberano

Brandy, 36% ABV

DISTILLERY Gonzalez Byass, Jerez de la Frontera, Spain. Spirit launched in 1913.

PHILOSOPHY Having played a leading role in the world of Spanish brandies, this producer draws upon years of experience and knowledge of oenology (the study of wine).

The spirit High-quality Airen grapes pass through continuous distillation. The resulting spirit is aged using the Solera and Criadera system—a process through which distillate is aged in wine and sherry barrels.

The taste Amber–mahogany in appearance, this fragrant brandy wows the palate with smooth, elegant notes of oak, prunes, and raisins.

Van Ryn's 12 Year

Brandy, 38% ABV

DISTILLERY Van Ryn's Distillery, Western Cape, South Africa. Founded in 1845.
PHILOSOPHY This leading distillery continues to build on the namesake founder's philosophy—"excellence in maturation."

The spirit Chenin Blanc and Colombard grapes are harvested, then fermented to become a crisp, fruity wine. The team distills the spirit twice in small copper pot stills, then ages it in oak in cool, dark cellars. Finally, the brandy is blended.

The taste This golden brandy is spicy and fruity on the nose. The liquid yields flavor notes of fruit cake, oranges, and ripe tropical fruit.

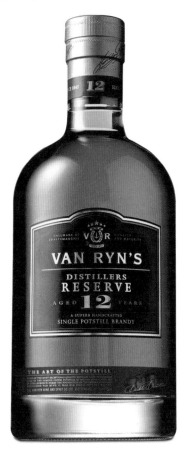

Ziegler No. 1 Wildkirsch

Eau de vie, 43% ABV

DISTILLERY Gebr. J. M. Ziegler GmbH, Baden-Wuerttemberg, Germany. Founded in 1865.
PHILOSOPHY This historic producer keeps an eye on the future of distilling, without forgetting traditional values.

The spirit The team harvests wild cherries by hand from trees that are up to 55ft (15m) tall. The cherries—33lb (15kg) of which go into each bottle—are then fermented and distilled in copper boilers. The eau de vie is then aged for three to five years.

The taste The fragrant, floral nose gives way to bright, fruity cherry notes. The long, smooth finish is zesty to some palates, and mild to others.

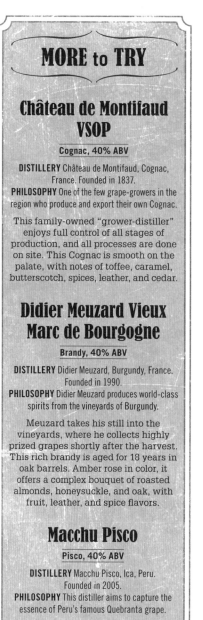

MORE to TRY

Château de Montifaud VSOP

Cognac, 40% ABV

DISTILLERY Château de Montifaud, Cognac, France. Founded in 1837.
PHILOSOPHY One of the few grape-growers in the region who produce and export their own Cognac.

This family-owned "grower-distiller" enjoys full control of all stages of production, and all processes are done on site. This Cognac is smooth on the palate, with notes of toffee, caramel, butterscotch, spices, leather, and cedar.

Didier Meuzard Vieux Marc de Bourgogne

Brandy, 40% ABV

DISTILLERY Didier Meuzard, Burgundy, France. Founded in 1990.
PHILOSOPHY Didier Meuzard produces world-class spirits from the vineyards of Burgundy.

Meuzard takes his still into the vineyards, where he collects highly prized grapes shortly after the harvest. This rich brandy is aged for 18 years in oak barrels. Amber rose in color, it offers a complex bouquet of roasted almonds, honeysuckle, and oak, with fruit, leather, and spice flavors.

Macchu Pisco

Pisco, 40% ABV

DISTILLERY Macchu Pisco, Ica, Peru. Founded in 2005.
PHILOSOPHY This distiller aims to capture the essence of Peru's famous Quebranta grape.

Quebranta grapes are grown solely in Peru; these are pressed gently to extract juice without bitterness from the skins. The single-distilled spirit rests for one year before bottling. This is crystal clear with a herbal nose and complex flavors of pear, sweet cream, and pepper, and a dry, fruity finish.

Infuse brandy and Cognac with complementary flavors. Try dried fruit, which becomes a sweet, boozy treat after the infusion. You can also infuse with the same fruit (for instance, apples in apple brandy), or play with various combinations. Follow the step-by-step technique on pages 24–25.

Pear

A pear-infused brandy works well in autumnal cocktails.

What you need 2–3 ripe pears, cored and cut into chunks; 3 cups brandy or Cognac.

Infusing time 1–2 weeks.

The next level Toss in a cinnamon stick or two for a great flavor pairing.

Dried Apricot

Bite-sized dried apricots are a perfect option when infusing almost any kind of brandy.

What you need 2lb (900g) dried apricots; 3 cups brandy or Cognac.

Infusing time 3–4 weeks.

The next level Add ½ vanilla pod or a cinnamon stick to lessen the infusion's fruit-forward expression.

Apple

Most bottles of apple brandy and Calvados respond well to an apple infusion.

What you need 2–3 ripe apples, cored and cut into chunks; 3 cups brandy or Cognac.

Infusing time 1–2 weeks.

The next level Add in any combination of dried cloves, allspice, and a cinnamon stick for a spiced infusion.

Cherry

Cherries impart a sweet–tart note to a brandy infusion.

What you need 1lb (450g) fresh whole cherries, stems removed; 3 cups brandy or Cognac.

Infusing time 2–3 weeks.

The next level Use 1 tbsp dried cloves or allspice to add a herbal note of flavor.

Prune

Infusing with dried prunes yields boozy fruit that you can eat or use as a garnish for cocktails.

What you need 1lb (450g) pitted prunes; 3 cups brandy or Cognac.

Infusing time 3–4 weeks.

The next level Add in a handful of other dried or dehydrated fruits—try fig or slices of pear or apple.

Walnut

Infuse roasted walnuts into a young, gentle brandy or Cognac to impart a rich, nutty flavor.

What you need 9½oz (280g) walnuts, toasted in a preheated oven at 350°F (180°C) for 5–10 minutes; 3 cups brandy or Cognac.

Infusing time 2–3 days.

The next level Add a handful of dried fruit, such as currants or golden raisins, for added depth.

Sidecar

The Sidecar first appeared in a cocktail manual in 1922, and rose in prominence in Europe during the '20s and '30s. Aficionados spent much of the twentieth century arguing over the perfect Sidecar—some insisted on a drier expression, while others preferred a sweeter finish. Find out where you stand with your own adaptation of the cocktail.

The Classic Recipe

A proper Sidecar should straddle the sweet–sour divide, allowing the flavor of Cognac to shine through.

1 Moisten the outer rim of a chilled coupe glass with a slice of lemon and coat it lightly with refined sugar. Pour 1fl oz (30ml) Cognac into a shaker.

2 Add ¾fl oz (20ml) orange liqueur.

3 Add ¾fl oz (20ml) fresh lemon juice. Add ice cubes, and shake for 10 seconds. Strain into the chilled coupe glass.

Serve it up Garnish with a lemon twist.

Create Your Own Signature Mix

Key Components

1 Pour **1fl oz (30ml) Cognac** into a shaker.

Basic Cognac can produce sweet results, so for a more balanced approach try a richer variety of the spirit. You can also replace it with Armagnac, fruit brandy, or bourbon.

2 Add ¾fl oz (20ml) **orange liqueur**.

The variety of orange liqueurs—from bitter and floral to sugary sweet—gives you many flavor options.

3 Add ¾fl oz (20ml) **fresh lemon juice**. Add ice cubes, and shake for 10 seconds. Strain into your glass.

Fresh lemon juice is best. For a sour experience, add a touch of lemon juice and pinch the lemon twist over the drink before consuming. Replace with orange juice and a twist for more sweetness.

Fresh lemon juice

Orange liqueur

Cognac

Additional Flourishes

Garnish Instead of a classic lemon twist, jazz things up with crystallized lemon peel or a slice of dehydrated lemon.

Sugar rim Try a heavier coating of sugar for sweet flavor, or go for flavored sugar, such as vanilla or lavender. You could also add ground cinnamon or ginger to the sugar.

Craft Reinventions

The Sidecar is a perfectly malleable cocktail. Mixologists often replace Cognac with Armagnac or bourbon, and introduce sweet fruit juices and bitters to complement the sweet–sour flavor profile. Here are three variations to try.

Le Sidecar du Armagnac

In a shaker, combine the Armagnac, liqueur, juice, and bitters. Add ice, and shake for 10 seconds. Strain into a chilled coupe, garnish with the lemon twist, and serve.

lemon twist
2 dashes orange bitters
2 tbsp fresh lemon juice
1 tbsp orange liqueur
2fl oz (60ml) Armagnac

Bourbon Tangerine Sidecar

Coat the rim of a chilled coupe with with refined sugar (see p29). Shake the liquid ingredients with ice in a shaker for 10 seconds. Strain into the glass, garnish with the twist, and serve.

tangerine twist
1 dash citrus bitters
1fl oz (30ml) fresh tangerine juice
1 tbsp fresh lemon juice
¾fl oz (20ml) orange liqueur
1¾fl oz (50ml) bourbon

◀ Autumnal Apple Sidecar

Coat the rim of a chilled coupe with refined sugar and cinnamon (see p29). Shake the liquid ingredients with ice in a shaker for 10 seconds. Strain into the glass, top with apple, and serve.

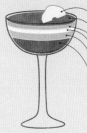

slice of dehydrated apple
1 dash spiced bitters
1 tbsp apple cider
1 tbsp fresh lemon juice
¾fl oz (20ml) orange liqueur
1½fl oz (45ml) apple brandy, such as Calvados

Vieux Carré

The Vieux Carré is a boozy cocktail named after the famous French Quarter in New Orleans. Walter Bergeron of the historic Hotel Monteleone created it in the late 1930s, and the recipe remains largely unchanged. Some ingredients are tricky to source, but are worth the effort. Play with unique interpretations of this glamorous favorite.

The Classic Recipe

A meeting of four strong yet distinct liquors, this delightfully complex cocktail is not for the booze-averse.

1 Pour 1fl oz (30ml) Cognac or brandy into a mixing glass.

2 Add 1fl oz (30ml) rye whiskey.

3 Add 1fl oz (30ml) sweet vermouth.

4 Add 1 teaspoon Bénédictine, and 1 dash each Peychaud's and Angostura bitters.

5 Fill the mixing glass with ice and stir with a bar spoon until the mixture is cold. Strain into a chilled ice-filled double old-fashioned glass. Serve.

Create Your Own Signature Mix

Key Components

1 Pour **1fl oz (30ml) Cognac or brandy** into a mixing glass.
For sweeter flavors, try a craft fruit brandy, such as apple or pear.

2 Add **1fl oz (30ml) rye whiskey**.
You could also try a sweeter, more mellow whisky instead of rye.

3 Add **1fl oz (30ml) sweet vermouth**.
This helps to temper the cocktail's alcohol-forward characteristics. For a drier result, swap it out for dry vermouth, or try a 50:50 ratio.

4 Add **1 teaspoon Bénédictine**, and **1 dash each Peychaud's and Angostura bitters**.
French Bénédictine liqueur is a must for many. You could also try Chartreuse or sweet Drambuie. Complex bitters also add spicy and sweet flavor notes.

5 Stir with a bar spoon until the mixture is cold. Strain into a chilled **ice-filled** glass.
For a change from the usual ice cubes, use just one large ice cube to ensure minimal melting and dilution.

Ice cubes

Bénédictine and bitters

Sweet vermouth

Rye whiskey

Cognac or brandy

Additional Flourishes

Garnish To complement the drink's herbal notes, add a sprig of fresh herbs, such as culinary lavender, juniper, or thyme.

Decorate For pretty results, top with some crystallized flower petals, such as violet.

Craft Reinventions

Mixologists create new versions of the Vieux Carré while remaining respectful to the classic. With fresh fruit or tart citrus juices to mitigate, the results are usually smoother and easier to drink. Here are three craft recipes to try.

Nouveau Carré

Pour the liquid ingredients into a mixing glass. Fill it with ice, and stir until cold. Strain into an ice-filled double old-fashioned or chilled coupe glass. Top with the twist, and serve.

- lemon twist
- 2 dashes Peychaud's bitters
- 1 tsp Bénédictine
- ¾fl oz (20ml) Lillet Blanc
- 1½fl oz (45ml) aged tequila

Apple–Pear Vieux Carré

Pour the liquid ingredients into a mixing glass. Fill it with ice and stir until cold. Strain into a ice-filled double old-fashioned or chilled coupe glass. Top with the twist, and serve.

- lemon twist
- 2 dashes Peychaud's bitters
- 1 tbsp fresh apple juice
- 1 tbsp fresh pear juice
- 1 tbsp fresh lemon juice
- 1 tsp Bénédictine
- 1 tbsp sweet vermouth
- ¾fl oz (20ml) each apple and pear brandy

◀ Tart and Sweet Honeymoon

Pour the liquid ingredients into a mixing glass. Fill it with ice, and stir until cold. Strain into a double old-fashioned or chilled coupe glass. Top with rosemary and lemon, and serve.

- rosemary sprig and slice of lemon
- 2 dashes lemon bitters
- 1 tbsp fresh lemon juice
- 1 tbsp Bénédictine
- 1 tbsp orange liqueur
- 2fl oz (60ml) apple brandy

Pisco Sour

The Pisco Sour is the national cocktail of Peru, and was created at the Victor Morris bar in Lima in the early 1900s. Today it is served in many ways, but the ingredients remain largely unchanged. When executed with skill, the Pisco Sour can convert anyone to the use of egg whites in cocktails. Create exciting and modern variations of this frothy favorite.

The Classic Recipe

The trick is to shake the drink twice—first without ice, then with. This yields the highly prized extra-frothy texture.

1 Pour 2fl oz (60ml) Peruvian pisco into a shaker.

2 Add ¾fl oz (20ml) fresh lime juice.

3 Add 1 tablespoon simple syrup.

4 Add 1 medium egg white. Shake for 15 seconds. Add ice, and shake again for 10 seconds. Strain into a chilled coupe or double old-fashioned glass.

Serve it up Garnish with three dashes of Angostura bitters.

Create Your Own Signature Mix

Key Components

1 Pour **2fl oz (60ml) Peruvian pisco** into a shaker.

Pisco has become popular all over the world, so there are now many varieties to explore. Try aromatic and non-aromatic varieties, or blends of both.

2 Add **¾fl oz (20ml) fresh lime juice**.

Lime juice cuts through the sweet brandy and sugar, and the rich egg. Try using key lime juice (as they do in Peru), or try lemon juice instead of lime.

3 Add **1 tablespoon simple syrup**.

Simple syrup helps to smooth out the cocktail's stronger characteristics.

4 Add **1 medium egg white**. Shake for 15 seconds. Add ice, and shake again for 10 seconds. Strain into your chilled glass.

The drink's frothy texture is due to the egg white. Replace it with powdered versions, but for the frothiest results, nothing works better than the real thing.

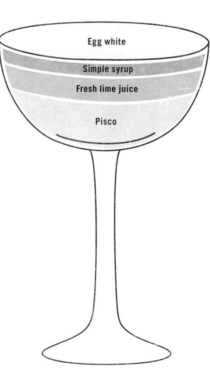

Egg white

Simple syrup

Fresh lime juice

Pisco

Additional Flourishes

Garnish Add a visual kick with a crystallized lime peel or dehydrated lime slice.

Bitters Try different flavors—from sweet fruits to tart citrus—to add another dimension to the drink.

Craft Reinventions

A Pisco Sour without the pisco or egg is an entirely different beast. That said, mixologists create fantastic variations—most feature an added flavor such as a fresh fruit or spice. On the right are three alternatives to add to your repertoire.

Spicy Passionfruit Pisco Sour

Combine the pisco, pulp, syrup, egg white, and juice in a shaker. Shake for 15 seconds. Add ice, shake again for 10 seconds. Strain into a chilled coupe. Sprinkle with chili powder, and serve.

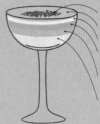

chili powder
1 tbsp fresh lime juice
1 medium egg white
¾fl oz (20ml) simple syrup
¾fl oz (20ml) passionfruit pulp
1¾fl oz (50ml) pisco

Grappa Sour

Combine grappa, juice, syrup, and egg white in a shaker. Shake for 15 seconds. Add ice, shake again for 10 seconds. Strain into a chilled coupe. Garnish with bitters, and serve.

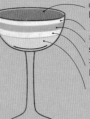

dash of Angostura bitters
1 medium egg white
¾fl oz (20ml) simple syrup
¾fl oz (20ml) fresh lemon juice
1¾fl oz (50ml) grappa

◀ Chilean Pisco Sour

Combine the pisco, ice, sugar, and juice in a blender. Blend for 30–45 seconds until frappé-like. Pour into a chilled coupe or double old-fashioned glass, top with bitters and the cherry, and serve.

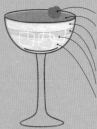

maraschino cherry
dash of Angostura bitters
1fl oz (30ml) fresh lemon juice
2 tbsp powdered sugar
4 medium ice cubes
2½fl oz (75ml) Chilean pisco

The Corpse Reviver No. 1 is a go-to "hair of the dog" hangover cure. According to the Savoy Cocktail Handbook from 1933, the drink should "be taken before 11am, or whenever steam or energy is needed." This version is richer and stronger than the gin-based No. 2. Whether or not you need the pick-me-up, this drink is ripe for reinvention.

The Classic Recipe

This remedy delivers a straight boost of booze, with sweet ingredients to soften the hit.

1 Pour 2fl oz (60ml) Cognac into a mixing glass.

2 Add 1fl oz (30ml) Calvados, or any apple brandy.

3 Add 1fl oz (30ml) sweet vermouth.

4 Fill with ice cubes, stir with a bar spoon until the mixture is cold, then strain into a chilled coupe glass.

Serve it up Garnish with a maraschino cherry or orange twist (optional).

Create Your Own Signature Mix

Key Components

1 Pour **2fl oz (60ml) Cognac** into a mixing glass.

Use a fruitier Cognac for a sweet flavor, or a dry one to balance the other ingredients.

2 Add **1fl oz (30ml) Calvados**, or any apple brandy.

This cocktail is sweet and strong. To soften the blow, replace the brandy with fresh apple juice.

3 Add **1fl oz (30ml) sweet vermouth**.

To balance the sweetness of the drink, replace this with a tablespoon each of dry and sweet vermouth.

4 Fill with **ice cubes**, stir until cold, then strain into your glass.

If you wish to dilute the drink's strength, give it an extra-long stir to allow for the ice to melt a little.

Sweet vermouth

Calvados

Cognac

Additional Flourishes

Garnish A sweet garnish, such as a slice of orange or maraschino cherry, gives your palate a welcome change.

Water You could add a few dashes of chilled water to dilute the strength.

Craft Reinventions

Most bartenders lighten the concentrated alcohol flavors with their recipes. Many add chilled water, or introduce new ingredients, such as sparkling wine or grenadine to dilute the spirits. Here are three creative recipes to try.

Mint Corpse Reviver

In a mixing glass, combine the brandy, crème de menthe, and Fernet Branca. Add ice, and stir until the mixture is cold. Strain into a chilled coupe, and serve.

1fl oz (30ml) Fernet Branca

1fl oz (30ml) white crème de menthe

1fl oz (30ml) brandy

Armagnac Corpse Reviver

In a shaker, combine the brandy, vermouth, Armagnac, juice, and bitters. Add ice, and shake for 10 seconds. Strain into a chilled coupe. Garnish with the cherry, and serve.

maraschino cherry

2 dashes Angostura bitters

1fl oz (30ml) fresh lemon juice

1fl oz (30ml) Armagnac

1fl oz (30ml) sweet vermouth

1fl oz (30ml) apple brandy

◀ Sparkling Corpse Reviver

In a shaker, combine the brandy, juices, and grenadine. Add ice, and shake for 10 seconds. Strain into a coupe or flute. Top with sparkling wine, garnish with the raspberry, and serve.

raspberry

sparkling wine

1 tbsp grenadine

1fl oz (30ml) fresh orange juice

1fl oz (30ml) fresh lemon juice

1½fl oz (45ml) apple brandy

The agave spirits family—tequila and its cousins mezcal, sotol, raicilla, and bacanora—are distilled from **desert plants** in Mexico. These spirits convey a true **sense of place**, as the rich volcanic soil in Mexico is required for the plants to **thrive**. The spirits are increasingly popular with drinkers **all over the world**. Craft producers are now creating good-quality versions that are often aged just like whiskies and rums—perfect for **sipping neat**. Fashionable mezcal, which is made from a wide variety of agave varietals, is generally noted for its aggressive, **spicy flavors**, and sotol, made from the desert spoon plant, is one of the most **expressive** varieties. With this chapter as your guide, you can embrace a wide range of agave spirits. You can even try infusing spirits with **flavor**, or **reinventing** the classic Margarita and Paloma cocktails.

AGAVE
SPIRITS

123 Organic Blanco

Tequila, 40% ABV

PRODUCER 123 Spirits, Jalisco, Mexico. Founded in 2010.
PHILOSOPHY Owner David Ravandi was inspired to design a tequila with wine enthusiasts in mind.

The spirit Agave hearts are roasted in a traditional stone oven for 48 hours, then undergo an all-natural fermentation for three to four days. The producer distills the agave hearts in both copper and stainless steel pot stills. The bottles are made from recycled materials.

The taste Unaged and clean, this tequila contains intense aromas of fresh agave. Vibrant flavor notes include lemon peel, black pepper, and minerals.

Amarás Espadín

Mezcal, 40.7% ABV

DISTILLERY San Juan del Río, Oaxaca, Mexico. Spirit launched in 2010.
PHILOSOPHY Through its devotion to the cultural roots of Mexico, this traditional distillery supports sustainable production.

The spirit At 10 years old, espadín agave is harvested and roasted in a conical stone oven. The team adds it to an Egyptian mill and ferments it in a pinewood container before double-distilling it in copper pot stills.

The taste You can detect touches of bergamot and blossom on the nose, giving way to flavor notes of sandalwood and matured mango.

Bosscal Joven

Mezcal, 42% ABV

DISTILLERY Bosscals 42 Agaves Distillery, Durango, Mexico. Spirit launched in 2013.
PHILOSOPHY This small producer pays respect to the Mexican people, culture, and traditions.

The spirit A fourth-generation *mezcalero* (distiller) cooks "silvestre" agaves for four days in earth ovens lined with volcanic rock. He crushes and grinds them by hand, leaves them to ferment naturally for two days, then distills them in stainless steel stills.

The taste This complex spirit is tart and sweet at the same time—just like passionfruit—with light notes of banana, kiwi, and blood orange.

Casa Dragones Joven

Tequila, 40% ABV

DISTILLERY Casa Dragones, Jalisco, Mexico. Founded in 2008.
PHILOSOPHY This small-batch producer uses new equipment to push the boundaries of tequila while shaping the industry for the future.

The spirit This sustainable, state-of-the-art process includes multiple distillations in an advanced column process, which reduces any harsh alcohol notes. The water is from natural aquifers 230ft (70m) deep so is enriched with minerals from the volcanic soil.

The taste This spirit offers brilliant platinum hues and a long, pronounced mouthfeel. The fresh, floral aroma elevates the flavors of vanilla and pear.

Cabeza

Tequila, 43% ABV

DISTILLERY El Ranchito Distillery, Jalisco, Mexico. Spirit launched in 2012.
PHILOSOPHY This family has been cultivating agave for five generations. They produce a versatile, field-to-bottle single-estate tequila, created for the bartending community.

The spirit The family cooks mature agaves in brick ovens for 24 hours, at which point fermentation is kick-started with champagne yeasts. The distillation occurs in a two-part, two copper pot still process. Finally, the tequila rests in stainless steel for 60 days before bottling.

The taste A true "growers' tequila," this is complex and agave-forward with notes of bitter citrus and black pepper.

Chinaco Blanco

Tequila, 40% ABV

DISTILLERY Tequilera La Gonzalena, Tamaulipas, Mexico. Founded in 1977.
PHILOSOPHY The first tequila distillery in the state of Tamaulipas paved the way for the modern tequila revolution.

The spirit This 100 percent agave tequila is bottled five days after distillation for a fresh taste. The agave is farmed at 5,000ft (1,500m) in local soil that is enriched with mineral content.

The taste The liquid carries a lovely bouquet of pear, quince, dill, and lime, followed by a smooth, lingering finish.

Clase Azul Reposado

Tequila, 40% ABV

DISTILLERY Productos Finos de Agave, Jalisco, Mexico. Spirit founded in 1997.
PHILOSOPHY This producer is inspired by a mission to reveal and rediscover a deeper appreciation for the beauty of Mexican traditions.

The spirit Blue agave is slow-cooked in traditional stone ovens for a minimum of 72 hours, then fermented and distilled. The spirit is then aged for eight months in oak barrels. Each bottle is handmade and hand-painted by Mexican artisans.

The taste With an intense amber color and rich body, this expressive spirit gives off aromas of earth, vanilla, and toffee caramel. On the palate, you can detect a wood-like note of cooked agave.

Del Maguey Vida

Mezcal, 42% ABV

PRODUCER San Luis del Rio, Oaxaca, Mexico. Spirit launched in 2010.
PHILOSOPHY The visionary Ron Cooper introduced the world to previously unavailable, 100 percent certified organic, artisanal mezcal produced using ancient and original organic processes.

The spirit As with Del Maguey's full product line, Vida is made by an individual family *palenquero* (producer) in an old-style village. Espadín agave is distilled in a copper still.

The taste The soft aromatic nose of roast agave, tropical fruit, and honey gives way to tastes of ginger, cinnamon, burnt sandalwood, banana, and tangerine, with a long and soft finish.

Fidencio Clásico

Mezcal, 45.5% ABV

DISTILLERY Fabrica del Amigo del Mezcal, Oaxaca, Mexico. Spirit launched in 2007.
PHILOSOPHY *Maestro Mezcalero* (Master Distiller) Enrique Jiménez is a fourth-generation distiller. As a farmer, he oversees the entire process.

The spirit Estate-grown agave espadín is roasted over black oak embers for five days, then ground and fermented for 6–12 days. The spirit is distilled two times and bottled at batch proof, without water.

The taste This sipping mezcal has delicate wood smoke and green pepper aromas and tastes of pipe tobacco, grilled pineapple, sage, and pine needles.

Hacienda de Chihuahua Añejo

Sotol, 38% ABV

DISTILLERY S.A. de C.V., Chihuahua, Mexico. Spirit launched in 1997.
PHILOSOPHY This acclaimed producer applies traditional methods to wild-harvested Agavacea (a member of the agave family, native to the Chihuahuan desert) to produce an authentic Sotol.

The spirit In a remote corner of the Chihuahuan Desert that is accessible only by donkey, the team hand-harvests sotol plants. The plants are steam-cooked for three days, champagne-yeast fermented, double-column distilled, and aged in Cognac barrels.

The taste This expressive spirit begins with a nose of toasted oil. The barrel influence provides elements similar to a rich brandy, and there's a distinctive agave flavor.

Leyenda Guerrero

Mezcal, 45% ABV

DISTILLERY Mezcales de Leyenda Distillery, Guerrero, Mexico. Founded in 2008.
PHILOSOPHY Working with single village and small Mexican producers to bring traditional mezcal to the limelight.

The spirit Hearts of agave (known as papalote) are roasted in a lava rock-lined pit, then mashed and fermented in open-air wooden vats. After 7–14 days, the spirit is double-distilled in a copper still.

The taste This rich and layered mezcal achieves great balance and style. Notes of roasted mango, smoked nuts, and peppercorns delight the senses.

Los Siete Misterios Tobalá

Mezcal, 48.3% ABV

DISTILLERY Palenque Los Siete Misterios, Oaxaca, México. Spirit launched in 2010.
PHILOSOPHY Made using only traditional methods, this distiller is proud to represent Mexican customs, culture, and passion.

The spirit Mature Tobalá agave hearts cook for three to five days in an earthen oven heated by river stones. The agave is then ground with wooden mallets to achieve a rough, thick paste. A two-stage distillation completes the process.

The taste Clean and bright, this mezcal carries notes of bitter chocolate, tar, tobacco, and dried plums, with hints of flowers and nutmeg on the finish.

Partida Blanco

Tequila, 40% ABV

DISTILLERY Tequila Partida Distillery, Tequila, Mexico. Founded in 2004.
PHILOSOPHY This boutique producer combines ancient production methods and modern technology to create authentic tequila from 100 percent blue agave.

The spirit Mature agave is slowly baked in steel ovens for 20–24 hours, and is then distilled twice—once to purify the fermented liquid, and then once more to achieve the right balance. The distillery bottles each one by hand.

The taste A crisp, floral nose with notes of citrus gives way to a burst of pure agave flavor and a pleasant finish that lingers gently on the palate.

Riazul Añejo

Tequila, 40% ABV

DISTILLERY Compañia Tequilera de Arandas, Jalisco, Mexico. Spirit launched in 2008.
PHILOSOPHY Transforming 100 percent blue agave into a progressive spirit that delivers a distinctive sense of place.

The spirit Mature agave plants are cooked through a hydrolysis process in stainless steel autoclaves, then fermented, distilled twice in a copper pot still, and aged in French oak for two years.

The taste Vibrant aromas of banana cake and frosting, maraschino cherry, and spicy pineapple compote give way to a fruity body with great depth of flavor.

San Cosme

Mezcal, 40% ABV

DISTILLERY Casa Legendaria, Oaxaca, Mexico. Spirit launched in 2011.
PHILOSOPHY Representing contemporary Mexico in a respectful way, this mezcal has been made using both traditional and modern techniques.

The spirit This old artisanal process has remained untouched for seven generations. The spirit is 100 percent espadín agave. The agave is cooked slowly in earthen ovens, then shredded (using horsepower) and fermented. The producer distills the spirit twice in copper pots.

The taste Scents of agave, smoke, wood, and humid earth give way to mouth-coating flavors of smoky agave, with a sweet yet citric finish.

Siembra Valles Blanco

Tequila, 40% ABV

DISTILLERY Destileria Cascahuin, Jalisco, Mexico. Spirit launched in 2014.
PHILOSOPHY This producer is dedicated to sustainability and quality and spreads knowledge and respect for Mexico's emblematic spirits.

The spirit The production team roasts agaves in brick ovens for 72 hours, then ferments them for 42 hours. They are distilled first in a 420-gallon (1,900-liter) stainless steel still, and then again in a 75-gallon (350-liter) copper still.

The taste The spirit coats the mouth with dry spices, dates, figs, floral notes, and copper tones straight from the still.

Tapatio Blanco

Tequila, 40% ABV

DISTILLERY La Alteña Distillery, Arandas, Mexico. Founded in 1937.
PHILOSOPHY One of the last Mexican family-owned Tequila distilleries, it uses Old World methods to ensure maximum flavor and the smoothest body.

The spirit The staff bakes 100 percent blue agave for four days, then crush and press it in a mill. They then ferment the agave with a 75-year-old yeast culture. It is double-distilled, filtered, and rests for six months.

The taste The lush, full-bodied spirit smells of rose, geranium, and pansy. It has a lively natural agave sweetness.

MORE to TRY

Cielo Rojo Blanco

Bacanora, 42% ABV

DISTILLERY Tepúa Distillery, Sonora, Mexico. Spirit launched in 2010.
PHILOSOPHY The family have been making Bacanora since the mid-1800s, and share the fruit of their cultural ancestry.

Mature wild agave (maguey bacanora) is harvested, cooked in firewood pits, and shredded. After 5–10 days of natural fermentation, it is distilled. Balanced and pleasant, this has wildly complex notes of stone fruit, ripe cactus, and burnt marshmallow.

Por Siempre

Sotol, 45% ABV

DISTILLERY Compania Elaboradora de Sotol, Chihuahua, Mexico. Spirit launched in 2015.
PHILOSOPHY This sixth-generation distillery honors tradition by using wild-harvested sotol.

Sotol is sourced from nearby mountain slopes. Pit-roasting and open-air fermentation imparts smoke and earth flavors, preserved by two distillations. Taste elements of black pepper and wet stone, and the rich mouthfeel turn into a long, dry, and mildly smoky finish.

La Venenosa Costa

Raicilla, 45.5% ABV

DISTILLERY La Goroupa, Cabo Corientes, Jalisco, Mexico. Founded in 2009.
PHILOSOPHY Achieving a historic flavor profile by using traditional equipment and practices.

Agave Rhodacantha is harvested at 8–10 years old, then roasted for three days, and milled by hand. After fermentation, the spirit distills twice in a hollowed-out tree trunk. This spirit has strong, savory flavor notes of green olives, cedar, and campfire.

Infusing Agave Spirits

Of all agave spirits, tequila is the best choice for infusing—some mezcals are a little too spicy. For flavour combination ideas, think of all the Margarita varieties out there. As with any spirit, taste your chosen bottle first to register the primary flavor notes, and then infuse by following the instructions on pages 24–25.

Jalapeño

This spicy infusion works well with agave spirits.

What you need
2–3 medium jalapeños, deseeded and sliced; 3 cups agave spirit.

Infusing time 1–2 days.

The next level Balance the heat from the peppers with sweetness by adding 1 tbsp agave syrup.

Watermelon

Perfect for festive tequila drinks, watermelon provides a natural sweetness that negates the spirit's aggressive flavors.

What you need 1 small watermelon (seedless, if available), peeled and cut into chunks; 3 cups agave spirit.

Infusing time 5–7 days.

The next level If your melon is very ripe, add some jalapeño or cucumber slices to tone down the sweetness.

Pineapple

Sweet pineapple provides a natural complement to lighter agave spirits.

What you need
1 pineapple, peeled and cut into chunks; 3 cups agave spirit.

Infusing time 5–7 days.

The next level Add ½ vanilla pod or a few jalapeño slices to add a different flavor note.

Cucumber

Infusing any spirit with cucumber yields a fresh, clean note.

What you need
2 cucumbers, ribboned with a peeler; 3 cups agave spirit.

Infusing time 1–2 days.

The next level A few slices of fresh chile pepper gives a fresh and spicy result.

Strawberry

When making a strawberry Margarita, use this infused tequila for a natural sweetness.

What you need 1lb 2oz (500g) fresh strawberries, stems removed; 3 cups agave spirit.

Infusing time 3–5 days.

The next level A sliced cucumber tempers some of the sweetness; and a few jalapeño slices creates a sweet–spicy infusion.

Lime

If you always garnish tequila with fresh lime, try infusing it with lime peel.

What you need Peel of 10 limes, pith removed; 3 cups agave spirit.

Infusing time 3–5 days.

The next level Add 1 tbsp agave syrup to counterbalance the acidity of the lime.

Margarita

The Margarita is the most famous tequila cocktail. It is thought to date from late 1930s Mexico. Today, consumers drink millions of nondescript Margaritas that feature mixes to cover up cheap tequila. However, mixologists now feature craft tequilas in exciting and innovative Margarita variations—these ideas will inspire you to join in.

The Classic Recipe

Creating a classic Margarita from scratch is far more rewarding—and delicious—than using a bland mix.

1 Rub the rim of a Margarita or coupe glass with a lime wedge. Rim the glass by placing it face-down on a plate covered with coarse sea salt. Set aside.

2 Pour 2fl oz (60ml) tequila into a shaker.

3 Add 1fl oz (30ml) triple sec.

4 Add 1fl oz (30ml) fresh lime juice. Add ice cubes, and shake for 10 seconds.

5 Fill your glass with crushed ice. Strain the shaker into the glass.

Serve it up Garnish with a lime wedge.

Create Your Own Signature Mix

Key Components

1 Rub the rim of your glass with a lime wedge, and place it rim-down on a plate covered with **coarse sea salt**.

To ring the changes, you can add a dash of salt into the drink. Try smoked or pink Himalayan salt.

2 Pour **2fl oz (60ml) tequila** into a shaker.

Use an unaged craft tequila here, as it is a shame to mask an aged variety with sweet flavors.

3 Add **1fl oz (30ml) triple sec**.

You could opt for something less sweet, such as brandy or orange extract.

4 Add **1fl oz (30ml) fresh lime juice**. Add ice cubes, and shake for 10 seconds.

Along with salt, lime juice is a key partner of tequila.

5 Fill your glass with **crushed ice**. Strain into the glass.

Crushed ice keeps the drink super-cold and tasting fresh.

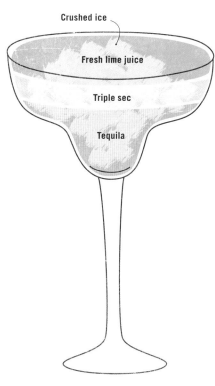

Crushed ice

Fresh lime juice

Triple sec

Tequila

Additional Flourishes

Fruit Add mango, strawberry, and peach—simply swap out the triple sec for fresh purée or juice and add a garnish.

Frozen For a different texture, add your preferred recipe to the blender, add a few ice cubes, and blend until it is smooth and silky.

Spice Tequila pairs with spicy flavors. Muddle a fresh jalapeño in your shaker before adding the ingredients, or try a chili-powder rim.

Craft Reinventions

The classic rocks-and-salt Margarita has been updated and refreshed by many a mixologist. You can easily swap trendy mezcal in for tequila, or explore exotic fruit flavors—moving the drink away from its saccharine past.

Mango Strawberry Margarita

Pour the tequila, triple sec, bitters, juices, and ice to a shaker. Shake for 10 seconds. Strain into a crushed ice-filled coupe glass. Garnish with a strawberry and wedge of lime. Serve.

strawberry and lime wedge

1fl oz (30ml) mango juice
1 tbsp fresh lime juice
2 dashes citrus bitters
1 tbsp triple sec
2fl oz (60ml) tequila

Smoky Spicy Mezcal Margarita

Rim a coupe glass with smoked salt (see p29) and fill with ice. Pour the liquid ingredients and ice cubes into a shaker. Shake for 10 seconds and strain into the glass. Top with the lime, and serve.

lime wedge
1fl oz (30ml) lime juice
1 tsp honey
2 dashes of spicy bitters
2fl oz (60ml) mezcal

◀ Watermelon Margarita

Rim a coupe glass with sea salt (see p29) and fill with ice. Pour the liquid ingredients and ice into a shaker. Shake for 10 seconds. Strain into the glass, top with the fruit, and serve.

lime wedge and sliced kumquat

1fl oz (30ml) watermelon juice
1 tbsp fresh lime juice
1 tbsp triple sec
2fl oz (60ml) tequila

Paloma

The Paloma, which translates from Spanish into "dove," is the most popular cocktail in Mexico. The simple drink pairs tequila with citrus fruit—a marriage that brings out the best in the spirit. Reinvent this Mexican favourite by serving your own interpretation of a refreshing, authentic, and remarkably easy Paloma cocktail.

The Classic Recipe

This original features a salt-rimmed glass and fizz from soda water.

1 Rub the rim of a collins glass with a grapefruit slice. Place the glass rim-down on a plate covered with medium-ground sea salt. Set aside.

2 Pour 2fl oz (60ml) tequila into a shaker.

3 Add 3fl oz (90ml) fresh ruby red grapefruit juice.

4 Add 3fl oz (90ml) soda and ice cubes, and shake for 10 seconds.

5 Fill the collins glass with ice cubes, and strain the mixture into it.

Serve it up Garnish with a grapefruit slice.

Create Your Own Signature Mix

Key Components

1 Rub the rim of your glass with a grapefruit slice. Place the glass rim-down on a plate covered with **medium-ground sea salt**.

For extra flavor, try smoked salt.

2 Pour **2fl oz (60ml) tequila** into a shaker.

Some prefer a mellow blanco tequila, but others will find an aged tequila more enjoyable. Spicy mezcal also holds up well in this drink.

3 Add **3fl oz (90ml) fresh ruby red grapefruit juice**.

For a slightly bitter flavor, replace this with fresh pink grapefruit juice.

4 Add **3fl oz (90ml) soda** and ice cubes, and shake for 10 seconds.

Add sliced cucumber to your soda to impart a cool, refreshing taste.

5 Fill your glass with **ice cubes**, and strain the mixture into it.

For a hint of spice, add a dash of hot sauce or chili powder to your water ahead of freezing.

Salt rim

Ice cubes

Soda

Red grapefruit juice

Tequila

Additional Flourishes

Bitters For added grapefruit punch, add a dash of grapefruit bitters.

Garnish Add a slice of white grapefruit for a naturally bitter flavor. Pink or red grapefruits are a sweeter choice.

Herbs Palomas pair nicely with a number of fresh herbs—try a sprig of rosemary, thyme, or basil.

Craft Reinventions

From switching out tequila for mezcal to ramping up the sweet or spicy notes, there are many ways to reimagine the Paloma. On the right are three of the best interpretations of this Mexican favorite.

Spicy Mezcal Paloma

Rim a collins glass with sal de maguey (see p29) and fill with ice. Pour the liquid ingredients and ice into a shaker. Shake for 10 seconds. Strain into the glass, top with grapefruit, and serve.

- slice of grapefruit
- 3fl oz (90ml) soda
- 3fl oz (90ml) white grapefruit juice
- 2 dashes spiced bitters
- 2fl oz (60ml) mezcal

Salt and Honey Paloma

Rim a collins glass with smoked salt (see p29) and fill with ice. Pour the liquid ingredients and ice into a shaker. Shake for 20 seconds and strain into the glass. Add the grapefruit. Serve.

- slice of grapefruit
- 3fl oz (90ml) soda
- 1 tbsp honey
- 2 dashes honey bitters
- 3fl oz (90ml) white grapefruit juice
- 2fl oz (60ml) tequila

◀ Jalapeño Paloma

Rim a collins glass or jar with sea salt (see p29). Fill it with ice. Muddle the chile and bitters in a shaker. Add the liquid ingredients and ice. Shake for 10 seconds, strain, and top with chile. Serve.

- slice of jalapeño
- 3fl oz (90ml) soda
- 3fl oz (90ml) white grapefruit juice
- 2fl oz (60ml) tequila
- 2 dashes spicy bitters, muddled with 4 slices of jalapeño

When it comes to spirits, ingredients, flavors, and techniques vary all over the world. Thanks to production and shipping advancements, we can now enjoy liquors such as **baijiu** (from China) and **cachaça** (from Brazil) in every corner of the planet. Enjoy Nordic **aquavit** or Japanese **shochu** on their own, or use them to lend an exotic note to myriad cocktails. **Vermouth** is a key component of classic cocktails but now craft producers are creating versions of such **quality** that they can be enjoyed neat. The bottles in this chapter (from an intense-flavored **absinthe** to an elegant **créme de violette**) are beloved by the world's greatest bartenders, who are always seeking something **unusual**. Follow in their footsteps and try for yourself—either sip it straight, mix up a balanced infusion, or reinvent the classic cocktails.

ABSINTHE, BAIJIU, AND MORE

Amaro delle Sirene

Liqueur, 29% ABV

DISTILLERY Don Ciccio & Figli, Washington D.C., USA. Founded in 2012.
PHILOSOPHY This distillery's range of handcrafted spirits demonstrates a love and respect for Italian artisanal liqueurs.

The spirit Based on a recipe from the Amalfi Coast that had not been produced since 1931, this handcrafted spirit features an infusion of 30 selected roots and herbs. The base spirit is made from corn and barley.

The taste This tobacco-hued and bitter spirit exudes aromas of eucalyptus, stewed ripe fruit, licorice, and rhubarb.

Amaro Lucano

Liqueur, 28% ABV

DISTILLERY Amaro Lucano S.p.A., Basilicata, Italy. Founded in 1894.
PHILOSOPHY One of Italy's most beloved liqueurs remains unchanged. Only members of the Vena family—currently on its fourth generation—participate in the final stages of production to ensure continuity and confidentiality.

The spirit This secret recipe uses more than 30 local herbs and spices to create a caramel-brown spirit that is primarily enjoyed as a digestif after a meal.

The taste This liqueur has a bittersweet flavor that is packed with a kaleidoscope of botanical notes.

HOW TO ENJOY Enjoy this chilled and neat, with an orange peel.

Amaro Sibilla

Liqueur, 34% ABV

DISTILLERY Distilleria Varnelli, Macerata, Italy. Founded in 1868.
PHILOSOPHY This historic distillery is run by a family—four women of its fourth generation run it today, upholding traditions of crafting by hand.

The spirit The producers use an age-old secret recipe of native herbs and plants. The ingredients are ground with a mortar and pestle, then heated over log-fueled fires and sweetened with honey. A long aging and decanting period completes the process.

The taste This smooth-tasting, moderately bitter spirit offers aromas of bitter herbs, dried fruit, chestnuts, and walnuts, followed by scents of coffee and honey.

Averell Damson Gin

Liqueur, 33% ABV

DISTILLERY The American Gin Company, New York, USA. Spirit launched in 2010.
PHILOSOPHY This bold liqueur reaps the benefits of the seasonal damson plum harvests in New York State.

The spirit Damson plums are a unique ingredient in the world of liqueurs—they have concentrated flavors, notes of spice, astringency in their skin, and high acidity in their flesh. The producers press and juice the plums, then blend them with small-batch American gin.

The taste Bright and acidic, this liqueur is packed with the essences of sweet fig and prune, with a punch of warm winter spice.

Artemisia La Clandestine

Absinthe, 53% ABV

DISTILLERY Artemisia Distillerie, Val-de-Travers, Switzerland. Founded in 2005.
PHILOSOPHY In the village where absinthe was born, this producer uses a Swiss housewife's recipe that dates back to 1935.

The spirit The staff macerates local plants—including wormwood and hyssop—in distilled neutral grain alcohol. The liquid is re-distilled in copper stills and reduced with mountain stream water.

The taste An initial honey sweetness gives way to mild bitterness. Fresh floral notes include rose petals and mint.

Avuá Amburana

Cachaça, 40% ABV

DISTILLERY Fazenda da Quinta Ltda., Rio de Janeiro, Brazil. Spirit launched in 2013.
PHILOSOPHY To use the traditional values of cachaça production and honor indigenous Brazilian ingredients and materials.

The spirit This single-estate producer grows sugar cane in a long and remote valley. The team ferments freshly pressed cane juice with wild yeast. The ferment is then pot-distilled and aged for two years in vats made from Amburana, a Brazilian wood that is often used for cachaça.

The taste An intriguing mix of warm and savory notes run the gamut from cinnamon and winter spices to mint.

Belsazar Rosé

Vermouth, 17.5% ABV

DISTILLERY Alfred Schladerer Hausbrennerei, Staufen im Breisgau, Germany. Spirit launched in 2014.

PHILOSOPHY This producer is rooted in tradition while uniquely using German high-quality wines.

The spirit Up to 20 spices, herbs, peels, and blossoms are macerated and mixed with wine from the South Baden region. After filtering, the spirit matures in stoneware casks for up to three months.

The taste This bittersweet spirit yields tones of grapefruit, orange blossoms, bitter orange, raspberries and red currants.

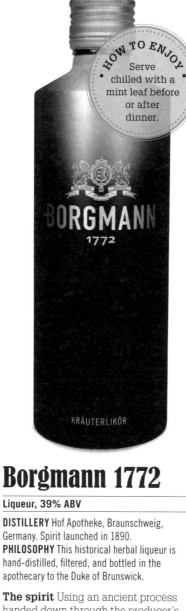

HOW TO ENJOY Serve chilled with a mint leaf before or after dinner.

Borgmann 1772

Liqueur, 39% ABV

DISTILLERY Hof Apotheke, Braunschweig, Germany. Spirit launched in 1890.

PHILOSOPHY This historical herbal liqueur is hand-distilled, filtered, and bottled in the apothecary to the Duke of Brunswick.

The spirit Using an ancient process handed down through the producer's family, each bottle is made from a mix of hand-picked medicinal and aromatic plants. The liqueur is cooled while it ages, and then filtered in small batches.

The taste Brown in color, this spirit offers fleeting notes of cinnamon, cloves, bitter orange, and cinchona bark.

Byrrh Grand Quinquina

Liqueur, 18% ABV

DISTILLERY Caves Byrrh, Thuir, France. Founded in 1866.

PHILOSOPHY Producing perhaps the most famous French apéritif wine, this distillery upholds their original methods and traditions.

The spirit This producer macerates a secret mix of herbs and spices into the *mistelles* (a slightly fermented white wine to which brandy has been added) and wines of Roussillon. This is then aged for up to one year.

The taste With an almost juicy mouthfeel, this complex spirit features spicy and mildly bitter elements.

Cocchi Torino

Vermouth, 16% ABV

DISTILLERY Giulio Cocchi, Cocconato d'Asti, Italy. Founded in 1891.
PHILOSOPHY To maintain the methods of the founder, Giulio Cocchi—a young pastry chef who was fascinated with the pairing of food and wine.

The spirit One of only two vermouths with PDO status (the other being Dolin Vermouth de Chambéry), this uses fine Moscato wine as its base, infusing it with a secret recipe of botanicals.

The taste This vermouth has aromas of singed orange peel, vanilla, and caramel. Bitter, earthy flavors are balanced by sweeter notes of licorice and orange.

Clear Creek Moscato

Grappa, 40% ABV

DISTILLERY Clear Creek Distillery, Oregon, USA. Founded in 1985.
PHILOSOPHY One of America's foremost craft distilleries is renowned for using locally sourced fruit and European techniques.

The spirit Making use of Oregon's strong viniculture, this producer distills the pressed skins and seeds (the pomace) of fine local Muscat grapes to produce a sophisticated American grappa.

The taste This very floral spirit is smooth and pleasant, with notes of honeysuckle and lemon mid-palate, and a clean finish.

Crispin's Rose

Liqueur, 25.4% ABV

DISTILLERY Greenway Distillers, California, USA. Spirit launched in 2007.
PHILOSOPHY To invigorate consumers' palates with exceptional, creative spirits.

The spirit The producers macerate rose petals into an apple–honey eau de vie; after a short period of time the petals are strained out. All of the spirit's color and flavor comes from the roses.

The taste Delicate and floral, this lightly sweet liqueur gives off notes of caramel, brandy, and spice, with some tannins present on the finish.

Dolin Rouge

Vermouth, 16% ABV

DISTILLERY SAS Dolin, Chambéry, France. Founded in 1821.
PHILOSOPHY This producer creates Vermouth de Chambéry that has protected designation of origin (PDO) status—the only vermouth in France with this recognition.

The spirit This light and fresh spirit is made from a maceration of herbs and spices, which are married into a base of Ugni Blanc wine. The color comes from the plants, and from sweetening with dark, caramelized sugar.

The taste This is a gentle, lightly floral vermouth. Less sweet than its red Italian counterparts, there are notes of dried fruit and honey.

Duplais Verte

Absinthe, 68%

DISTILLERY Oliver Matter AG, Kallnach, Switzerland. Spirit launched in 2005.
PHILOSOPHY Using prestigious nineteenth-century distilleries as role models, this producer creates an authentic spirit.

The spirit Duplais is based on a recipe from a French book that was originally published in 1876. A specialized Swiss farm grows specific botanicals exclusively for the spirit, which is distilled in 1920s' copper pot stills.

The taste This golden-green liquid offers clear notes of wormwood and fennel, with a rich, creamy mouthfeel and long finish.

Green Chartreuse

Liqueur, 54% ABV

DISTILLERY Voiron, Rhône-Alpes, France. Founded in 1764.
PHILOSOPHY Chartreuse monks produce the only green liqueur in the world with a completely natural green color.

The spirit This spirit is made in the Grande-Chartreuse Monastery using the original process and secret formula—only the monks know the 130 herbs in the recipe. The spirit matures for several years in 100-year-old oak barrels.

The taste An initial honey sweetness gives way to a mild bitterness. Fresh floral notes include rose petals and mint.

HOW TO ENJOY Mix this with Champagne, gin, or vodka.

Iichiko

Shochu, 25% ABV

DISTILLERY Iichiko Hita Distillery, Ōita, Japan. Spirit launched in 1978.
PHILOSOPHY This producer uses traditional methods to create a quality spirit, the name of which translates into "fine" or "good" in the Ōita Japanese dialect.

The spirit This producer ferments steamed barley wheat using koji mold, then twice-malts it with malt, yeast, and soft local water. The liquid is then stored in a tank, and mixed with water and several unblended whiskies.

The taste A rich yet gentle spirit, Iichiko gives a fresh and fruity flavor, featuring deep umami notes.

Hyakunen no Kodoku

Shochu, 40% ABV

DISTILLERY Kuroki Honten, Kyushi, Japan. Founded in 1885.
PHILOSOPHY This organic, self-sustaining producer is a trailblazer of the industry, introducing many new expressions of shochu.

The spirit This *honkaku* ("genuine" or "authentic") shochu is made from an organic cereal base, which is distilled once in pot stills. Aging lasts for five years in sherry barrels.

The taste Amber in color, this spirit has a strong flavor of barley.

Jade 1901 Absinthe Supérieure

Absinthe, 68% ABV

DISTILLERY Combier, Saumur, France. Spirit launched in 2006.
PHILOSOPHY Making accurate recreations of original, authentic absinthes—without the use of modern ingredients or industrial equipment.

The spirit The absinthe historian T. A. Breaux uses modern science to reverse-engineer recipes for historic absinthes. He makes Jade 1901 using botanicals, grape eau de vie, and pot stills that were used in the nineteenth century.

The taste This vintage-style absinthe is balanced and crisp, with a stimulating herbal aroma and finish.

Jade 1901 Absinthe Supérieure is a genuine Belle Époque-style absinthe made at the historic Combier Distillery in Saumur, France. It was the inspiration of American expert T. A. Breaux to reverse-engineer the recipe for this authentic spirit from antique absinthe bottles.

What's the story?

In 2000, Breaux became the first person to use modern scientific methods to analyze samples of absinthe taken from sealed antique bottles. Using this analysis, Breaux created a recipe for Jade 1901.

In line with his historic focus, Breaux distills at the Combier Distillery, which is owned by Franck Choisne. Originally founded in 1834, the distillery was expanded by Gustave Eiffel in the late-nineteenth century. With Eiffel's signature ironwork intact, Combier is effectively a working museum. In addition to Jade's range of five craft absinthes, Breaux uses the distillery to produce a tobacco liqueur and pimento aromatic bitters.

Breaux distills to exact specifications, employing nineteenth-century materials and crafting methods. These laborious efforts include procuring whole herbs cultivated from their original regions, and resting distillates for up to several years before bottling. Some botanicals are so difficult to obtain commercially that the distillery now runs its own farm.

Above Jade Liqueurs' logo includes the fleur-de-lis. This reflects Breaux's French ancestry—his family originates from the same locale as the Combier Distillery.

Above Two different cultivars of absinthe's namesake herb, *Artemisia absinthium*, grow at the Combier Distillery's private farm.

Left Antique copper pot stills are lined up in an iron framework created by Gustave Eiffel, of Eiffel tower fame.

Who is behind it?

The Founder and President of Jade Liqueurs, **T. A. Breaux**, is a research scientist from New Orleans, who has actively studied absinthe for more than 20 years. Creating Jade 1901 in 2005—in an innovative collaboration with Combier Distillery owner Franck Choisne—was Breaux's attempt to boost a market that was then heavily saturated with green-colored vodkas posing as absinthe. In 2007, Breaux and New York lawyer Jared Gurfein managed finally to lift the longstanding US ban on absinthe, which had been introduced in 1912.

Breaux packs every last ounce of historical **authenticity** into the Jade **absinthe range**

FOUNDED IN
2000

2012 Awarded 4.5/5 by *Difford's Guide*

2012 Awarded 4.6/5 by **The Wormwood Society**

2007 SILVER MEDAL WINNER
at the **International Wine and Spirits Competition** in London, UK

Jian Nan Chun Chiew

Baijiu, 52% ABV

DISTILLERY Jian Nan Chun, Sichuan Province, China. Founded in 1998.

PHILOSOPHY With a heritage stretching back more than 1,200 years, this distillery preserves its ethos: to maintain its spirits' traditional characteristics of subtlety, purity, and refinement.

The spirit A mix of 50 percent sorghum and 50 percent mixed grains (rice, wheat, sticky rice, and corn) is fermented in earthen pits that have been in use for more than 300 years.

The taste This product stands apart from other "strong aroma" baijius due to its subtle, light sweetness (reminiscent of sugar cane), and its round, soft palate.

KINGS COUNTY DISTILLERY
moonshine
corn whiskey 200ml
40% alcohol by volume

Kings County Distillery Moonshine

Moonshine, 40% ABV

DISTILLERY Kings County Distillery, New York, USA. Founded in 2010.

PHILOSOPHY This upstart producer believes that unaged whisky is the raw expression of a distiller's talent.

The spirit The producer makes a sour mash from 80 percent organic cracked corn and 20 percent malted barley. The spirit is distilled twice in traditional pot stills from Scotland. Distilled water is added to reach a gentle proof, and there is no chill filtering, resting, or additives.

The taste This lightly hazy spirit smells of corn husks, with a bright and intense flavor that's heavy on corn.

Koval Orange Blossom

Liqueur, 20% ABV

DISTILLERY Koval Distillery, Illinois, USA. Founded in 2008.

PHILOSOPHY The owners of this distillery—the first to open in Chicago since the mid-1800s—left academic careers behind to make organic spirits.

The spirit This producer uses an award-winning white rye whiskey as the base—a unique idea that adds depth to the spirit. Floral orange blossom and sugar cane are added.

The taste Aromatic and sweet; flavors of orange blossom shine through.

Krogstad Festlig

Aquavit, 40% ABV

DISTILLERY House Spirits Distillery, Oregon, USA. Founded in 2004.
PHILOSOPHY Inspired by the great American cocktail gins of the pre-Prohibition era, this successful distillery produces an award-winning aquavit.

The spirit Traditional Scandinavian recipes have inspired this Swedish-style aquavit, which places an emphasis on star anise. Balanced and tasty, the unaged spirit is crafted from American grain spirit that is naturally gluten-free.

The taste This aquavit produces aromas and flavors of anise seed, rye bread, fennel, and allspice, with a soft, medium body.

Kuro Kirishima

Shochu, 25% ABV

DISTILLERY Kirishima Shuzo Co. Ltd., Miyazaki, Japan. Founded in 1916.
PHILOSOPHY This producer carves its own path by putting care into the production of its products, including this *imo* (sweet potato) shochu.

The spirit Made with a pair of highly prized ingredients—"Kogane Sengan" sweet potatoes and soft, underground water—this shochu gets its thick sweetness from the use of black koji rice.

The taste Richer than most barley- or rice-based shochus, this clear spirit has a warm mouthfeel, with complex, somewhat spicy, notes throughout.

Kweichow Moutai Feitian

Baijiu, 53% ABV

DISTILLERY Kweichow Moutai Distillery, Kweichow Province, China. Founded in 1704.
PHILOSOPHY This historic distillery creates one of the few baijius in the "complex aroma" category with the use of local water and microorganisms.

The spirit In 1951, this baijiu was officially recognized as the national liquor of the People's Republic of China. Unlike most traditional versions of the spirit, producers use only sorghum, and ferment it in stone pits. Aging occurs for at least three years before blending.

The taste This spirit sports a floral nose with notes of miso, gingko nuts, and burnt rice. The palate is dry and smooth with notes of toffee, coffee, and earth.

Linie

Aquavit, 41.5% ABV

PRODUCER ArcusGruppen, Gjelleråsen, Norway. Spirit launched in 1807.

PHILOSOPHY The company behind Norway's oldest and most prestigious aquavit produces this spirit in exactly the way it was over 200 years ago.

The spirit A potato-based spirit is aromatized with spice distillates, such as caraway, coriander, and star anise. Aging occurs in sherry oak barrels for 16 months—four of which occur at sea. The gentle, varying temperatures, rolling movement of the waves, and sea air enhance the flavors and are key in the maturation process.

The taste Light amber in color, the liquid gives off hints of orange peel, vanilla, oak, spices, and sherry.

This boat represents the vessel that, in 1807, returned from the East Indies with unsold aquavit on board. The voyage made an improvement to the flavor, which is why Linie is now always aged at sea

This is the signature of Jørgen B. Lysholm, the creator of Linie

Luzhou Laojiao Zisha

Baijiu, 52% ABV

DISTILLERY Luzhou Laojiao Distillery, Sichuan Province, China. Founded in 1573.

PHILOSOPHY This distillery—one of the oldest distilleries in China, from the time of the Ming Dynasty—aims to create spirits in the earthly world that are in harmony with the universe.

The spirit A mix of 60 percent sorghum, 20 percent wheat, and 20 percent rice ferments in pits—many of them original. The spirit is then distilled using a continuous still.

The taste This "strong aroma" baijiu smells of pepper, ripe peaches, and burnt rice. It has a slight sweet flavor, with notes of peach and pear.

Mãe de Ouro

Cachaça, 40% ABV

DISTILLERY Fazenda Mãe de Ouro Ltda., Minas Gerais, Brazil. Founded in 2002.
PHILOSOPHY Sharing Brazil's rich heritage with this handcrafted interpretation of the national spirit.

The spirit This producer harvests unburnt sugar cane by hand, then juices and ferments it. The ferment is distilled in a traditional copper pot still. Before bottling, the spirit is triple-filtered and aged in used bourbon oak barrels for at least one year.

The taste You can notice aromas and flavors of fresh meringue, plantain skin, Brazil nuts, dried tropical fruit, and banana leaf.

La Maison Fontaine Blanche

Absinthe, 56% ABV

DISTILLERY Distillerie Les Fils d'Emile Pernot, Pontarlier, France. Spirit launched in 2010.
PHILOSOPHY This classically produced absinthe—with a contemporary twist—gets its character from its home in Pontarlier, known as the "Absinthe capital of the world."

The spirit The producer macerates around 15 herbs overnight in a mix of distilled alcohol, then distills the liquid in a 200-gallon (900-liter) steam-heated unit—the oldest commercial absinthe still in the world.

The taste The sweet and refreshing flavor features rich floral notes with hints of lemon, mint, anise, and fennel.

Mizu (Mizunomai)

Shochu, 35% ABV

DISTILLERY Munemasa Shuzo Co., Saga, Japan. Spirit launched in 2013.
PHILOSOPHY Pairing creativity and innovation with a legacy of artisanship that stems from the town's rich tradition of fine porcelain crafts.

The spirit This producer creates a high-proof shochu by distilling a base of 67 percent locally farmed barley with 33 percent black koji rice in a stainless steel pot still. Only soft water from the nearby Black Hair Mountain is added.

The taste With aromas of cantaloupe and cut grass, there are flavor hints of banana, caramel custard, and vanilla. Black koji adds depth and richness.

Mizu Shochu (Mizunomai)

Mizu Shochu, or "Mizunomai", as it is known in its country of origin, is an authentic shochu (Japanese distilled spirit) made in the remote town of Arita, Japan. In a tradition preserved since the sixteenth century, fermented rice and polished barley are distilled only once to preserve the character and flavor of the ingredients.

What's the story?

The Munemasa family operated a small *kura* ("sake brewery") in Hiroshima until the devastation of the Second World War forced the brewery into bankruptcy. The family's ancestors were shochu distillers. Inspired by this, they founded Munemasa Shuzo Co. in Arita, Saga, in 1985.

The town is best known as the birthplace of fine Japanese porcelain, but the Munemasa *shuzo* ("distillery" or "brewery") is attracting attention for its products—shochu, sake, plum wine, and even craft beers—that celebrate provincial flavors and embrace the agricultural heritage of the area. The distillery prides itself on its close bond with the local farmers, sourcing all the ingredients from the area surrounding Arita.

Mizu Shochu is made from steamed rice coated with black koji—a microbe which helps break starch down into sugar—and barley that is polished to remove the husk. The resulting mash is distilled once and left to mellow for at least six months. The distillate is then filtered through bamboo charcoal and combined with water from nearby Kurokami-Yama (Black Hair Mountain).

Shochu has been distilled since the 1500s, and has gained new favor in the twenty-first century: it has outsold sake in Japan for the past decade, and shochu bars are particularly popular among the younger generation.

Above Arita's Tozan Shrine on a hilltop overlooking the town. It is dedicated to the founder of Arita-yaki porcelain and is said to bring good fortune to the local artisans. The Munemasa distillery lies a few miles south of the shrine, near the edge of the town.

The *genshu* ("distillate") ranges from
38–44% ABV

Mizu Shochu is made with roughly
1 part **black koji rice**
to 2 parts **barley**

Winner of Double Gold
at the **2013** New York World Wine & Spirits Competition

Left A mash of barley, rice, and occasionally sweet potato is distilled once in Munemasa's stainless steel pot still.

Below The label depicts two cranes, in reference to the name of the spirit, which translates as "dance of the beautiful cranes."

美鶴乃舞

mizu™
shochu

Who is behind it?

Munemasa's *toji* ("Master Distiller"), **Hirofumi Okoba**, has a profound understanding of the grains that make up the soul of his shochus, having grown up on a small family farm dedicated to growing barley and rice. Okoba maintains close friendships with many of his growers and believes that "shochu is something they make together," from the farm to the finished bottle.

Novo Fogo Silver

Cachaça, 40% ABV

DISTILLERY Agroecológica Marumbi, Paraná, Brazil. Spirit launched in 2010.
PHILOSOPHY This sugar-cane plantation and distillery in the rainforest produces a range of organic, sustainably crafted cachaças.

The spirit Fresh sugar-cane juice is fermented using native yeasts cultivated from the distillery's sugar-cane fields. The producer distills this ferment, then rests it in large stainless-steel tanks for one year.

The taste A pure representation of sugar cane and terroir, this cachaça carries rainforest notes of banana, sea salt, and sweet red pepper.

Nadeshiko

Shochu, 25% ABV

DISTILLERY Ikinokura Distillery, Akita, Japan. Founded in 1984.
PHILOSOPHY Using a traditional method that dates back more than 400 years, this producer honors Iki Island's rich history with shochu.

The spirit Nadeshiko ("True Beauty") shochu is made with a base comprising 67 percent barley and 33 percent rice. Cherry-blossom yeast gives the flavor a unique complexity.

The taste The spirit's alluring nose of cherries and floral notes leads into a bold flavor profile. Spicy alcohol notes battle with sweet cherry essence for attention.

La Quintinye Blanc

Vermouth, 16% ABV

DISTILLERY EuroWineGate Spirits & Wine, Cognac, France. Spirit launched 2014.
PHILOSOPHY A tribute to Jean-Baptiste de La Quintinye, a visionary who created the Kitchen Gardens at the Palace of Versailles.

The spirit The base is a blend of local wines, married with 18 botanicals and fortified with a grape-based neutral spirit. No sugar or caramel is added— the sweetness comes from the natural fructose of the grape juice.

The taste This spirit is packed with a bouquet of flavors, from vanilla to spicy botanical, with a long-lasting finish.

Rothman & Winter Crème de Violette

Liqueur, 20% ABV

DISTILLERY Destillerie Purkhart, Steyr, Austria. Founded in 1931.
PHILOSOPHY Creating the world's foremost violet liqueur, this distillery eschews the common practice of adding notes of vanilla and citrus.

The spirit The producer macerates aromatic roots, stems, and flowers, and then marries them into a grape-based alcohol. To achieve the finished product, the team add sugar, water, and color.

The taste A delightful, efficient tool for adding complex floral elements to a cocktail, this spirit balances a light sweetness with very mild acidity.

The label design and long bottle shape are influenced by Art Deco design—prevalent during the 1930s era when the distillery was founded

The color of the liqueur resembles wild violets that are native to the Alps, such as Queen Charlotte and March violets

Salers Gentian Apéritif

Liqueur, 16% ABV

DISTILLERY Distillerie des Terres Rouges, Turenne, France. Founded in 1885.
PHILOSOPHY Creating the oldest of the French Gentian Liqueurs—a handcrafted historical elixir that remains totally natural and specific to the distillery.

The spirit The roots of hand-harvested gentian—a yellow plant native to the local area—are macerated for weeks, before being separately distilled. The infusion and the distillate are blended, enriched with spices and herbs, and aged in Limousin oak barrels for months.

The taste With a distinctive bitterness, this spirit gives off a copious bouquet of herbal and citrus notes.

Shui Jing Fang Wellbay

Baijiu, 52% ABV

DISTILLERY Shui Jing Distillery, Sichuan Province, China. Spirit launched in 2000.
PHILOSOPHY Drawing on a unique wealth of yeasts that has been collected for over 600 years, the first baijiu distillery in China makes sure every drop tastes as it did during ancient dynasties.

The spirit The base of this "strong aroma" baijiu is made from a mix of grain—36 percent sorghum—that ferments in earthen pits for 30–90 days before steam distillation. The spirit ages for one to three years in a terra-cotta urn.

The taste The nose reveals fruity, floral aromas, with particular hints of plum. The refreshing, subtly sweet flavor hints of earth and moss.

Stählemühle Sicilian "Moro" (No. 239)

Liqueur, 42% ABV

DISTILLERY Edelobstbrennerei Stählemühle, Eigeltingen, Germany. Founded in 2004.
PHILOSOPHY This husband and wife team produces more than 200 varieties of fruit spirits by hand—mashing, distilling, and bottling.

The spirit Without adding sugar or additives—following the code of fruit distillers—this liqueur is produced using secret maceration and distillation techniques, with no chill-filtering. Sicilian Moro blood oranges form the base.

The taste A burst of orange greets the nose; on the palate there are spicy notes and a long and warming finish.

Tim Smith's Climax

Moonshine, 45% ABV

DISTILLERY Belmont Farm Distillery, Virginia, USA. Founded in 2010.
PHILOSOPHY The family of Master Distiller Tim Smith made moonshine illegally for over a century. Today, Smith proudly shares his spirit with the world.

The spirit Smith pot-distills the spirit slowly, using only locally grown ingredients (corn, barley, and rye). Water is not added, so that the spirit absorbs the flavors from the grains.

The taste Mildly sweet and gentle for a moonshine, this spirit's clean and natural characteristics are similar to those of a young whisky.

Velvet Falernum

Liqueur, 11% ABV

DISTILLERY Foursquare Distillery, Saint Philip, Barbados. Founded in 1920.
PHILOSOPHY This historic distillery produces the oldest surviving and most famous of Falernum, a blend of light rum with exotic spices and limes from the island of Dominica.

The spirit Spices and white rum are macerated in large vats; after this process, the spirit is filtered once, then blended with sugar and tart lime.

The taste This spirit gives off spice and citrus aromas, with a note of fresh cane from the white rum.

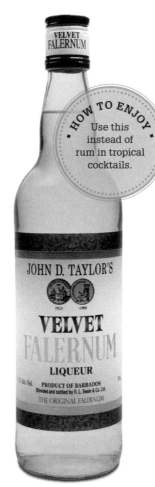

HOW TO ENJOY Use this instead of rum in tropical cocktails.

Vieux Pontarlier

Absinthe, 65% ABV

DISTILLERY Emile Pernot Distillery, Pontarlier, France. Founded in 2001.
PHILOSOPHY Dedicated to the glory of the well-made cocktail, this producer recreates rare spirits and liqueurs from the pages of history.

The spirit Made in the historic "Capital of Absinthe," this spirit uses select botanicals and the finest locally grown wormwood. The base spirit is made from Chardonnay grapes from Burgundy. The producer distills the spirit in antique alembic stills that are designed specifically for making absinthe.

The taste Pale green in color, this strong spirit exudes a fresh, slightly spicy aroma. Flavors of anise, fennel, and mint lead the charge.

MORE to TRY

Kronan Swedish Punsch

Liqueur, 26% ABV

DISTILLERY L.O. Smith, Götene, Sweden. Founded in 1993.
PHILOSOPHY A national drink in Sweden, this historic liqueur is a key component in classic cocktails.

The producer follows an age-old recipe—a historic combination of cane spirits of the East and West Indies, spices, and sugar. After the ingredients are blended in maceration tanks, the spirit rests for a few months, and is bottled. Perfect for an array of tiki drinks, this spirit carries complex flavors commonly found in rum.

Montanaro Barolo

Grappa, 43% ABV

DISTILLERY Distilleria Montanaro, Alba, Italy. Founded in 1885.
PHILOSOPHY This producer applies constant supervision throughout the entire production process to craft a historically accurate spirit.

Grape skins—sourced from the region's best wine producers—are kettle-steamed and distilled. The spirit ages for at least a year in oak barrels that are more than 100 years old. Soft and refined, this elegant, straw-colored grappa has a complex profile.

Suprema Refosco

Grappa, 41% ABV

DISTILLERY Fantinel Family, Pordenone, Italy. Founded in 2006.
PHILOSOPHY After years of research, the Fantinel family launched a line of spirits that embody the pinnacle of Friulian-style grappa.

The skins of Refosco dal Peduncolo Rosso—a local grape variety—are selected, then undergo a modern version of an ancient distillation process. Flavors of grapes, lemons, and almonds linger on the palate, with a stony, mineral quality on the finish.

Infusing Absinthe, Baijiu, and More

With care and consideration, you can infuse just about any spirit. If in doubt, it is best to infuse with a spirit's base ingredient, and in the process ramp up the intensity of those flavors. Here are adventurous infusions to try—for best results, follow the instructions on pages 24–25.

Chai and Sweet Vermouth

Many cocktails feature sweet vermouth—you can add complexity to each recipe by infusing the spirit with spicy chai tea bags.

What you need 3 chai tea bags; 3 cups sweet vermouth.

Infusing time 12–14 hours.

The next level Boost the herbal flavors by including 1 cinnamon stick and 1 tbsp cloves.

Pink Peppercorn and Baijiu

For a spicy expression of China's most popular spirit, infuse it with colorful pink peppercorns.

What you need 4 tbsp pink peppercorns; 3 cups baijiu.

Infusing time 1–2 days.

The next level Add one lemongrass stalk, split in half, to add a floral note to the infusion.

Fennel and Aquavit

Infusing Scandanavia's beloved Aquavit with fennel creates a Nordic taste sensation.

What you need 1 bulb fennel, sliced; 3 cups aquavit.

Infusing time 3–5 days.

The next level To complement the flavors, add a handful of fresh dill.

Ginger and Cachaça

Infusing a young cachaça with fresh ginger produces a wonderful base for a flavorful Caipirinha.

What you need 2-in (5-cm) piece fresh ginger; 3 cups cachaça.

Infusing time 5–7 days.

The next level Adding the peel from one lime or lemon adds a great tart flavor note to the infusion. Be sure to remove any bitter pith.

Pineapple and Cachaça

Pineapple provides a nice complement to this tropical spirit.

What you need 1 pineapple, peeled and cut into chunks; 3 cups cachaça.

Infusing time 5–7 days.

The next level Throw in a handful of jalapeño slices to spice up your infusion.

Peach and Moonshine

You can take some of the sting out of overproof moonshine and impart a sweet flavor by infusing it with ripe peaches.

What you need 2–3 peaches, quartered and pitted; 3 cups moonshine.

Infusing time 3–5 days.

The next level To sweeten further, add in 1 tbsp agave syrup or simple syrup.

Caipirinha

The Caipirinha is Brazil's most famous cocktail. When made correctly, just one sip can transport you to a sunny beach in Rio. The drink's origins are unknown, but it is thought that a version was used to treat Spanish Flu in the early twentieth century. With tart yet sweet flavors, the Caipirinha is a perfect playground for craft interpretation.

The Classic Recipe

Part of this drink's popularity is its simplicity—you need only three ingredients and a small amount of elbow grease.

1 Cut half of one large lime into quarters and place them in a double old-fashioned glass.

2 Add 2 teaspoons granulated sugar and muddle the ingredients together.

3 Fill the glass with crushed ice.

4 Pour over 2fl oz (60ml) cachaça, and lightly stir.

Serve it up Garnish with a lime wheel.

Create Your Own Signature Mix

Key Components

1 Cut half of **one large lime** into quarters and place them in your glass.

Fresh limes cut through cachaça's strong flavors. In Brazil, they use extra-tart key limes, but if you like sweeter flavors, try Tahitian limes.

2 Add **2 teaspoons granulated sugar** and muddle the ingredients together.

Use granulated sugar—it muddles well—and adjust quantities according to your taste. You could also try brown sugar for an earthier flavor.

3 Fill the glass with **crushed ice**.

Use finely crushed ice for this cocktail, as it melts quickly and dilutes the strength.

4 Pour over **2fl oz (60ml) cachaça**, and lightly stir.

Most recipes use aged cachaça, but unaged versions also work well. You could replace cahaça to make a Caipiroska (with vodka) or Caipiríssima (with rum).

Crushed ice

Cachaça

Granulated sugar

Lime

Additional Flourishes

Garnish For even more sourness, top with a lime wheel. To introduce spicy–sweet notes, try a slice of crystallized ginger.

Bitters You can add complementary flavors with a dash or two of tropical, tiki, or citrus-flavored bitters.

Muddle To introduce more flavors, muddle the lime with other ingredients, such as sliced cucumber or raspberries.

Craft Reinventions

Mixologists play with the classic recipe in lots of ways—often by simply adding tart or sweet fruits, or swapping out the base spirit for vodka or rum. Here are three modern recipes that turn this Brazilian favorite on its head.

Lychee Caipirinha

Add the sugar, lychees, and bitters to a double old-fashioned glass. Muddle. Add crushed ice, pour over the cachaça, and lightly stir. Top with the lychee, and serve.

- 1 canned lychee, drained
- 2fl oz (60ml) cachaça
- 2 dashes ginger bitters
- 2 canned lychees, drained
- 1 tsp granulated sugar

Grapefruit Mint Caipiroska

Lightly muddle the sugar, grapefruit, and mint in a shaker. Add ice, juice, and vodka, and shake for 10 seconds. Strain into an ice-filled double old-fashioned glass. Top with mint, and serve.

- mint sprig
- 2fl oz (60ml) vodka
- 1fl oz (30ml) fresh grapefruit juice
- 6 leaves fresh mint
- wedge of grapefruit
- 2 tsp brown sugar

◀ Clementine Caipirinha

Add the sugar, clementine, and bitters to a double old-fashioned glass. Muddle, and remove any pulp with a bar spoon. Add ice and cachaça, and stir. Garnish with the clementine, and serve.

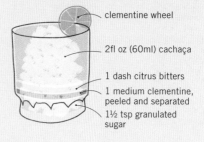

- clementine wheel
- 2fl oz (60ml) cachaça
- 1 dash citrus bitters
- 1 medium clementine, peeled and separated
- 1½ tsp granulated sugar

Negroni

The Negroni is a fashionable café favorite that has taken the world by storm. Hailing from 1920s Italy, this stylish cocktail is a light and easy-to-drink apéritif with a distinctive red color. It is made from equal parts of three simple ingredients—meaning it is easy to prepare, and just as easy to customize according to your preference.

The Classic Recipe

Often referred to as the world's greatest apéritif, the Negroni is the perfect way to serve Campari.

1 Pour 1fl oz (30ml) gin into an ice-filled mixing glass.

2 Add 1fl oz (30ml) Campari.

3 Add 1fl oz (30ml) sweet vermouth. Stir well with a bar spoon until cold.

4 Strain into an ice-filled double old-fashioned glass or a chilled Martini glass.

Serve it up Garnish with an orange twist.

Create Your Own Signature Mix

Key Components

1 Pour **1fl oz (30ml) gin** into an ice-filled mixing glass.

Negronis work best with a mild gin—botanical varieties are too strong. If you're a rum or tequila fan, replace the gin with an equal measure of either.

2 Add **1fl oz (30ml) Campari**.

Campari's bitter notes shine through. If you dislike Campari's unique flavor, consider sweeter alternatives, such as Cynar, Cardamaro, or Aperol.

3 Add **1fl oz (30ml) sweet vermouth**. Stir well with a bar spoon until cold.

The vermouth gives a sweet and rounded edge. You could swap it out for another fortified wine, such as sherry, or, if you have a sweet tooth, port.

4 Strain into an **ice-filled** double old-fashioned glass or a chilled Martini glass.

Ice dilutes the strength. If you want to keep the drink cold without dilution, choose the Martini glass, or use one large ice cube.

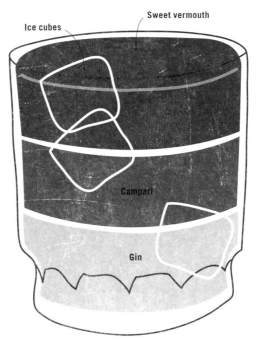

Ice cubes

Sweet vermouth

Campari

Gin

Additional Flourishes

Bitters The allure of a simple Negroni is strong, but you could add a dash of interesting bitters, such as maple or cinnamon.

Garnish The classic is served with an orange twist, but you could top with other citrus fruits, such as kumquat, or a sprig of rosemary.

Sparkle For a sparkling Negroni, add 1fl oz (30ml) sparkling wine and serve it in a tall collins glass.

Craft Reinventions

Bars serve a wonderful variety of Negroni cocktails. Many mixologists enjoy swapping the gin for different spirits—it is amazing how much impact mezcal can have on the flavor, for example. Here are three exciting versions to try.

Orange Negroni

Pour the liquid ingredients into an ice-filled mixing glass. Stir until the mixture is cold. Strain it into an ice-filled double old-fashioned glass, top with crystallized peel, and serve.

- crystallized orange peel
- 1 dash Peychaud's bitters
- 1 tbsp fresh orange juice
- 1fl oz (30ml) Campari
- 1fl oz (30ml) gin

White Negroni

Pour the gin, Suze, and Lillet Blanc into an ice-filled mixing glass. Stir for 20 seconds. Strain it into an ice-filled double old-fashioned glass, garnish with a lemon twist, and serve.

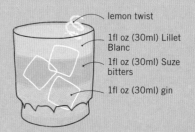

- lemon twist
- 1fl oz (30ml) Lillet Blanc
- 1fl oz (30ml) Suze bitters
- 1fl oz (30ml) gin

◀ Mezcal Negroni

Pour the liquid ingredients into an ice-filled mixing glass. Stir for 20 seconds. Strain into an ice-filled double old-fashioned glass. Rub the orange peel around the rim of the glass. Serve.

- round of orange peel
- 1fl oz (30ml) sweet vermouth
- 1 dash Angostura bitters
- 1fl oz (30ml) Campari
- 1fl oz (30ml) mezcal

Absinthe Frappé

The Absinthe Frappé offers a pleasant gateway to perhaps the most infamous of all spirits. It is said that absinthe—the "green fairy"—had grown so popular in nineteenth-century Paris that its unique scent hovered above the city's boulevards. Served super-cold to soften the aniseed flavor of the spirit, this palate-pleasing drink is perfect for those new to absinthe.

The Classic Recipe

Absinthe shines in this cocktail. Some purists question the need for simple syrup or mint, but there is one aspect that almost everyone agrees on: the need for crushed ice.

1 Pack a collins glass with crushed ice.

2 Add 8 mint leaves to a shaker.

3 Add 1 tablespoon simple syrup, and gently muddle.

4 Add 1½fl oz (45ml) absinthe and ice cubes, and shake for 15 seconds.

5 Strain into the glass, and top with 2fl oz (60ml) soda.

Serve it up Garnish with a sprig of mint.

Create Your Own Signature Mix

Key Components

1 Pack a collins glass with **crushed ice**.

The Frappé needs to stay very cold, so crushed or pebbled ice is a must.

2 Add **8 mint leaves** to a shaker.

For a cool and refreshing flavor, add 4 mint leaves with 3 slices of cucumber.

3 Add **1 tablespoon simple syrup**, and gently muddle.

Many enjoy absinthe straight with a sugar cube and a dash of cold water. Simple syrup blends very well in this cocktail, but try replacing it with 1 teaspoon refined sugar.

4 Add **1½fl oz (45ml) absinthe** and ice cubes, and shake for 15 seconds.

Make sure you use a real absinthe—there are countless modified products. If you're a fan of the flavor of absinthe, but not its strength, try substituting with a lower-proof pastis or an anise-flavored liqueur.

5 Strain into the glass, and top with **2fl oz (60ml) soda**.

Temper absinthe with soda water. You could also try a spring water flavored with lemon juice, or infusing soda water with fresh mint.

Crushed ice

Soda

Absinthe

Simple syrup

Mint

Additional Flourishes

Decorate For a fun spin, decorate your drink with a stick of rock sugar – either a classic brown sugar version, or a brightly colored one.

Garnish Mint complements absinthe's wormwood flavor very well— enhance your cocktail with a leaf or sprig.

Cream Some recipes add 1 tbsp heavy cream to the shaker with the absinthe and ice. This creates an impressive froth and smooth flavor.

Craft Reinventions

Bartenders give this drink wide appeal by mixing in new flavor components, such as sour lemon juice, refreshing mint, or savory ground almonds. For a fresh interpretation of the cocktail, give one of these three recipes a whirl.

Sour and Frothy Frappé

In a shaker, gently muddle the mint and syrup. Add juice, absinthe, egg white, and ice. Shake for 20 seconds. Strain into an ice-filled collins glass, top up with soda, and stir. Top with mint. Serve.

- mint sprig
- 2fl oz (60ml) lemon-infused soda
- 1 medium egg white
- 1½fl oz (45ml) absinthe
- 1 tbsp fresh lemon juice
- 1 tbsp simple syrup
- 6 mint leaves

Lime–Mint Absinthe Frappé

In a shaker, gently muddle the mint and syrup. Add juice, bitters, absinthe, and ice. Shake for 20 seconds. Strain into a crushed ice-filled collins glass, top up with soda, and stir. Top with mint. Serve.

- mint sprig
- 2fl oz (60ml) lime-infused soda
- 1½fl oz (45ml) absinthe
- 1 dash lime bitters
- 1fl oz (30ml) fresh lime juice
- 1 tbsp mint-infused simple syrup
- 10 mint leaves

◄ Almond Absinthe Frappé

In a shaker, add the absinthe, liqueur, syrup, juice, and ice. Shake for 20 seconds. Strain into a crushed ice-filled collins glass, top up with soda, and stir. Top with almonds. Serve.

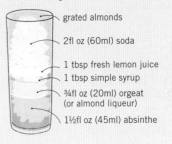

- grated almonds
- 2fl oz (60ml) soda
- 1 tbsp fresh lemon juice
- 1 tbsp simple syrup
- ¾fl oz (20ml) orgeat (or almond liqueur)
- 1½fl oz (45ml) absinthe

Index

Entries in **bold** indicate cocktail recipes.

About the Author

Eric Grossman is a spirits, dining, and travel writer based in Boston and New Orleans. He writes extensively about craft spirits and international cocktail trends, most notably for *USA Today*. He has visited numerous distilleries and judged cocktail competitions. Always eager to share his knowledge, Eric is a true ambassador for the craft spirits industry and is viewed as a "key influencer" by several liquor companies and branding agencies. EHGrossman.com

Acknowledgments

Eric Grossman would like to thank:
Brian Barrio, Tom Brady, Sharon Coppel, Scott Gastel, Chris Godleman, Armida Gonzalez, Ellen Grossman, Jeffrey Grossman, Grossman Family, Hayflick Family, Informed Diner supporters, Janne Johansson, Gerrish Lopez, Otto Lopez, Lopez Family, TK Gore, James Jackson, Jimmy Lynn, Chris Martin, Patrick McGee, Cheryl Patsavos, Alex Pember, Jim Raras, Brandon Ross, Richard Royce, Adam Salter, John Tierney, the entire DK team, and the world's finest producers, distillers, bartenders, and experts for their valued assistance.

DK would like to thank:
Photography: William Reavell. Photography art direction: Vicky Read. Recipe styling: Kate Wesson. Prop styling: Linda Berlin. Cocktail consultancy: Ed Thorpe. UK spirits consultant: Mark Ridgwell. Design assistance: Philippa Nash. Editorial assistance: Mickey Catelin, Mizue Kawai, Alice Kewellhampton, Mari Komoda, Tia Sarkar, and Amy Slack. Proofreading: Claire Cross. Indexing: Vanessa Bird.

Picture Credits

The publisher would like to thank all of the distilleries featured in the book for their kind permission to reproduce photographs. Thanks also to the following:

(Key: a-above; b-below/bottom; c-center; f-far; l-left; r-right; t-top)

11 The Library of Congress, Washington DC: (tl, br). 74 McHenry & Sons: Peter Jarvis (bc). 104 Osborne Images: (l). 134 Manulele Distillers: Ari Espay and Liza Politi (c). 159 n141.com: Stéphane Charbeau (tl). 160–61 n141.com: Stéphane Charbeau (all images). 179 Tequila Casa Dragones: (c). 183 Charbay Artisan Distillery and Winery: Fany Camarena (tl).

All other images © Dorling Kindersley
For further information see: www.dkimages.com